YA
B
Kel

Koestler-Grack,
Rachel A.,
1973-

Helen Keller.

Women of Achievement

Helen Keller

Women of Achievement

Abigail Adams

Susan B. Anthony

Tyra Banks

Clara Barton

Hillary Rodham Clinton

Marie Curie

Ellen DeGeneres

Diana, Princess of Wales

Helen Keller

Sandra Day O'Connor

Georgia O'Keeffe

Nancy Pelosi

Rachael Ray

Eleanor Roosevelt

Martha Stewart

Venus and Serena Williams

Women of Achievement

Helen Keller

ACTIVIST

Rachel A. Koestler-Grack

CHELSEA HOUSE
PUBLISHERS
An imprint of Infobase Publishing

HELEN KELLER

Chelsea House
An imprint of Infobase Publishing
132 West 31st Street
New York, NY 10001

Library of Congress Cataloging-in-Publication Data
Koestler-Grack, Rachel A., 1973–
Helen Keller: activist / by Rachel A. Koestler-Grack.
  p. cm. — (Women of achievement)
  Includes bibliographical references and index.
  ISBN 978-1-60413-502-2 (hardcover)
  1. Keller, Helen, 1880–1968. 2. Deafblind women—United States—Biography—Juve-
nile literature. 3. Deafblind people—United States—Biography—Juvenile literature. I.
Title. II. Series.
  HV1624.K4K644 2009
  362.4'1092—dc22
  [B]
                    2008055368

Series design by Erik Lindstrom
Cover design by Ben Peterson and Alicia Post

Printed in the United States of America

Bang EJB 10 9 8 7 6 5 4 3 2 1

This book is printed on acid-free paper.

All links and Web addresses were checked and verified to be correct at the time of
publication. Because of the dynamic nature of the Web, some addresses and links may
have changed since publication and may no longer be valid.

CONTENTS

Triumph over Silence

"Without language of some sort, one is not a human being," Helen Keller wrote in her autobiography *Midstream: My Later Life.* "Without speech, one is not a complete human being."[1] For the first 10 years of her life, Helen never spoke a clear word. The only sounds she uttered were meaningless noises, usually harsh and piercing, because it took her such great effort to make them. Helen was deaf and blind. When she was just a toddler, she became deathly ill. She survived but lost her ability to see and hear. As a child, she lived in a dark and silent world. No sunlight woke her in the morning. No voice stirred her quiet ears. She existed almost in a fog—unable to form words and thoughts, never feeling the tickle of true happiness.

All of that began to change when Helen was six years old. Annie Sullivan strolled up her front walk, ready to teach her. Sullivan opened up for Helen a whole new world, bursting with words, ideas, and emotions. Within three years, Helen could read and write better than many children her age who had not struggled with the challenges of blindness and deafness. She could even "listen" to people by placing her fingers on their lips and reading their movements and vibrations as they spoke. Her incredible achievements made her internationally famous. People around the world called her a "miracle child" and "the eighth wonder of the world." Helen was thrilled with her bright, enlightened life. She felt she was able to do many of the things that people who see and hear could do. Still, something was missing. She longed to talk like other people. She desperately wanted others to hear her speak.

Sullivan took Helen to Sarah Fuller, the principal of the Horace Mann School for the Deaf and one of the pioneering teachers of speech in the country. Fuller began to teach Helen how to speak. She started with the word *arm*, which Sullivan spelled into Helen's hand while Fuller said the word. Helen placed her hand on Fuller's face and felt the vibrations of her voice. Slowly and distinctly, Helen made the sound "ahm." She continued to imitate the sound, changing it ever so slightly, until Fuller was satisfied. That first day, Helen learned to speak several words in an airy, monotone voice.

In the following lessons, Fuller helped Helen improve her speech tones. She tried to make Helen understand that she must speak softly and not stiffen her throat or jerk her tongue. As hard as she tried, Helen had a difficult time making her voice sound natural. For someone who cannot hear, learning how to talk is strenuous and tiring. Helen's vocal cords had never been exercised for speech,

Helen Keller (*left*) posing with her doll and Annie Sullivan, the teacher who enabled her to learn despite the fact that Keller could not see or hear, while on vacation in Cape Cod, Massachusetts, in July 1888.

and controlling their movements took painful effort. The learning process was slow, but Helen refused to give up.

For nearly a decade, Helen had been mute, unable to utter a single word. Back then, mute people were referred to as "dumb." After just 11 lessons with Fuller, Helen was able to say, word by word, "I am not dumb now."[2] When Helen first started to speak, few people could understand her. Sometimes only Sullivan and Fuller knew what she was trying to say. After years of perseverance and determination, Helen was able to talk clearly enough for anyone to understand her. Helen's triumph over the silence that imprisoned her is hard for a seeing and hearing person to appreciate fully. Speech comes easily for someone who can hear. For a deaf person to learn natural speech, with its vast sounds, inflections, and tones, it is nothing short of a miracle.

OVERCOMING ADVERSITY

Although Helen Keller never achieved her lifelong dream of speaking completely clearly, she paved the way for others to learn how to do just that. Against overwhelming odds

IN HER OWN WORDS

Soon after her arrival, Annie Sullivan began to communicate with Helen Keller by spelling words into Helen's hands. Keller once said, as cited in *Helen's Eyes: A Photobiography of Annie Sullivan, Helen Keller's Teacher*:

> In her [Annie's] fingers words rang, rippled, danced, buzzed, and hummed. She made every word vibrant to my mind— she would not let the silence about me be silent.

and with unwavering perseverance, she grew into a highly intelligent and sensitive woman who wrote, spoke, and worked incessantly for the betterment of the disabled.

Keller changed the way people thought and felt about the deaf and blind all over the world. She said, "The public must learn that the blind man is neither genius nor a freak nor an idiot. He has a mind that can be educated, a hand which can be trained, ambitions which it is right for him to strive to realize, and it is the duty of the public to help him make the best of himself so that he can win light through work."[3]

From Light
into Darkness

To a child who has no sight or hearing, the pale blue sky on a sunny day, a vivid sunset of deep orange and red, the gold petals of a sunflower, the blare of a horn from a passing train, the trickling water of a stream, or a friend's contagious giggle mean nothing. Helen Keller could not enjoy the sight of a delicate swallowtail as it rested for a moment on the head of a daisy. She did not have the comfort of her mother's soothing voice when she was sick. But she did not always live in that strange, dark world. When she was born on June 27, 1880, she was a healthy child, possessing the ability to see and hear. Her mother named her Helen, which means "light," because she liked to imagine that her little girl's life would be carefree and full of brightness.

For almost two years, she lived like other children, playing in the sunshine on the lawn surrounding the Kellers' home, called Ivy Green, in Tuscumbia, a small, rural town in northwestern Alabama. Helen's mother, Kate, who was just 23 years old when Helen was born, doted on her daughter. Kate Adams had grown up in Tennessee, as a pampered southern belle. In 1879, she married 42-year-old Arthur H. Keller, a widower who had been a captain in the Confederate Army during the Civil War. Being nearly 20 years younger, Kate had little in common with her new husband, who had two grown sons from his first marriage. Kate got along quite well with the younger boy, a teenager, William Simpson. The older son, James, however, bitterly resented his new stepmother. When Helen was born, it must have been a relief for Kate. Now, she had her own child—someone to shower with love and affection.

According to Helen, the beginning of her life was simple and much like every other little life. "I came, I saw, I conquered, as the first baby in the family always does," she later recalled in her autobiography *The Story of My Life*.[1] At six months, Helen could call out, "How d'ye!" to visitors, and when she was thirsty, asked quite plainly for "Tea, tea, tea," or "wah-wah" for water.[2] On her first birthday, she took her first steps. Kate had lifted her out of the bathtub and was holding Helen on her lap when Helen was suddenly attracted to the flickering shadows of leaves swaying in the sunlight on the floor. Helen slipped down off her mother's lap and wobbled toward the dancing shadows. As soon as the impulse disappeared, she fell with a thud and burst into tears.

Those days of happiness and light did not last long. In February 1882, Helen was only 19 months old when she became severely ill with what doctors at the time called "brain fever." Her illness was most likely scarlet fever, a life-threatening disease that is caused by streptococcus bacteria. Some modern doctors believe Helen's symptoms could also have been caused by meningitis, an inflammation of the thin membranes that surround the spinal cord and brain. Whatever the mysterious illness, Helen's doctor thought that she would certainly die. Miraculously, Helen recovered and the Kellers breathed a sigh of relief. No one, though, not even the family doctor, knew that Helen would never see or hear again.

Years later, Helen could recall only broken fragments of her illness, which seemed more like a nightmare to her. Helen recalled the tenderness of her mother as she tried to soothe her sick daughter's agony and fear. She remembered her eyes being so dry and hot that she had to turn away from the light, which grew dimmer and dimmer each day. "I was too young to realize what had happened," Helen later wrote, according to *Helen Keller: A Life*, by Dorothy Herrmann. "When I awoke and found that all was dark and still, I suppose I thought it was night, and I must have wondered why day was so long coming. Gradually, however, I got used to the silence and darkness that surrounded me and forgot that it had ever been day."[3]

THE "LITTLE HOUSE"

In the South, many homes had a small cottage near the main house. At Ivy Green, Helen Keller's birthplace, the one-room cottage known as the "little house" was where Helen was born, and she lived there with her nurse until the time of her illness.

A recent photo of Ivy Green, Keller's childhood home in Tuscumbia, Alabama. The clapboard house was built in 1820.

STRUGGLES OF A NEW WORLD

With her sight and hearing gone, Helen had to learn how to live in a whole new kind of world—one without light and sound. The Kellers realized that Helen was not the same when she remained unresponsive after Kate passed her hand over Helen's eyes and Helen did not react to the dinner bell. Those first few months after her illness, Helen felt scared and alone. Terrified, she only wanted to sit on her mother's lap, and she clung to Kate's dress as she went about her household chores. Slowly, Helen began to venture out into the darkness, running her hands over objects and following motions with her fingertips. In this way, she learned to know what many things were.

Still, she felt the need for some kind of communication. She began to make crude signs as a way to talk. A shake of her head meant "no," and a nod was "yes." A pull meant "come" and a push "go." If she wanted a slice of bread, she would imitate the act of cutting slices and buttering them. When she wanted ice cream after dinner, she made the motions of working the freezer and shivered. Most of the time, Kate was able to understand Helen and rushed to give her whatever she wanted.

Because of Helen's severe disability, her parents could not bear to discipline her. As she grew older, she became extremely frustrated at not being able to communicate. Helen realized that she was different from other people, because her mother and her mother's friends communicated without signs when they wanted something. They talked with their mouths. Sometimes Helen stood between two people in a conversation and touched their lips while they talked. Helen would move her lips, but nothing happened. "This made me so angry at times that I kicked and screamed until I was exhausted," she later wrote in *The Story of My Life*.[4]

Helen was strong-willed and petulant. Her fits of rage and wild behavior terrorized the household. She deliberately broke dishes and lamps and stuck her hands into plates of food. Once she charged into the parlor in her red flannel underwear and repeatedly pinched her maternal grandmother until she chased the older woman from the room. Because Helen's disabilities prevented her from seeing or hearing people's reactions, she did not know that her actions were hurting her family. Some relatives called her "a monster," and one of them suggested that Helen be sent off to an institution.

Kate was overwhelmed by her challenges with Helen. She had adored her darling girl with soft, golden curls and

Helen Keller at age seven, around the time Annie Sullivan came to educate her.

pale blue eyes when she could see and hear. After Helen's illness, however, Kate began to feel guilty, frustrated, and helpless. She did not know how to deal with Helen's disruptive outbursts. Still, she refused to send her child away, no matter how desperate the situation became at home.

When Helen was five years old, Kate gave birth to a second girl, Mildred. In a fit of jealousy, Helen overturned her little sister's cradle, causing Mildred to fall out; had Kate not caught her as she tumbled out of her bed, Mildred might have died. In time, though, the sisters became friends. "Mildred and I grew into each other's hearts," Helen later

BELL'S TALKING DOG

Although best known for inventing the telephone, Alexander Graham Bell contributed much to the education of the deaf and blind. Despite being normally quiet and introspective as a child, he enjoyed experimenting in mimicry and "voice tricks" such as ventriloquism—the art of projecting one's voice so that it seems to come from another source, like a wooden figure. Bell was also deeply affected by his mother's gradual deafness (she began to lose her hearing when he was 12), and he learned a manual finger language so he could communicate with her. He also developed a technique of speaking in clear, precise tones, directly in front of his mother's forehead, in which she could understand him quite well. Bell's preoccupation with his mother's deafness led him to study acoustics—the scientific study of sound, especially of its generation, transmission, and reception.

Bell's family had an interest in the teaching of elocution, the art of public speaking. His grandfather, uncle, and father were all elocutionists. His father published a number of works on the subject, including *The Standard Elocutionist*. In this book, his father explained his methods of how to instruct deaf-mutes (as they were then known) to articulate words and read other wrote, "although she could not understand my finger language, nor I her childish prattle."[5]

FINDING HOPE

Day after day, Helen's desire to express herself grew. The few signs she had used as a child became less and less adequate. She felt trapped and desperately wanted to be understood. "I felt as if invisible hands were holding me,

people's lip movements. Bell's father taught him how to read lips. The boy was so proficient that he became a part of his father's public demonstrations. He astounded audiences with his abilities to read speech in other languages.

Bell's father encouraged his interest in speech. In 1863, he took Bell to see an automaton, or what would today be called a robot. This "mechanical man" could simulate a human voice. Bell was fascinated by the machine and afterward he and his older brother, Melville, built their own automaton head. Their remarkably lifelike head could "speak," even if it was only a few words. The boys would carefully adjust the lips and when one of them forced air through the mechanical windpipe, a very recognizable "mama" sound came out.

Pleased with his results, Bell continued to experiment—this time with a live subject, the family dog. After he taught it to growl continuously, he would reach into its mouth and manipulate the dog's lips. Eventually, he managed to produce a crude-sounding "Ow-ah-oo-ga-ma-ma." With a little convincing, he could make an audience believe his dog could speak the phrase "How are you, grandma?" Bell's talking dog experiment inspired his work to teach the deaf to speak.

and I made frantic efforts to free myself," she wrote years later.[6] Helen's outbursts became more and more frequent. By the time she was six years old, her fits of frustration erupted daily, sometimes hourly.

Helen's parents frantically searched for some way to help their daughter. In 1887, Kate found a ray of hope in a book by Charles Dickens, called *American Notes*. In the book, which was an account of his trip to North America in 1842, Dickens wrote about meeting a deaf and blind woman named Laura Bridgman, who had been taught to read and write. However, the man who had educated Laura, Dr. Samuel Gridley Howe, had died a decade earlier. Even if his teaching methods had been documented, who would come to far-off Alabama to teach her little girl? The Kellers lived far from any school for the blind and the deaf.

Kate and Arthur Keller took Helen to see numerous eye specialists in Alabama and Tennessee, but none of them could help the child. At last, one specialist arranged for them to meet with the famous ophthalmologist Dr. Julian Chisholm in Baltimore, who specialized in curing "hopeless" cases. At the consultation, the doctor told the Kellers that there was nothing medically that could be done to cure their daughter. In his opinion, though, they should not give up hope. He believed Helen could be taught, just like Laura Bridgman.

"There's a gentleman in Washington, a short distance away, who is an expert on the problems of deaf children," Dr. Chisholm explained. "Perhaps he can help you find a school or teacher for your little girl."[7] The man was Alexander Graham Bell, who had invented the telephone in 1876. Bell's interest in the deaf was not just scientific. His mother, Eliza, became deaf and could hear only with the help of an ear tube. His wife, Mabel, had lost her hearing at the age of five from scarlet fever. When Mabel was

16 years old, Bell became her private tutor, and they married several years later.

At Bell's office in Washington, the inventor picked Helen up and set her on his broad knee. He took out his pocket watch and placed it in her tiny hand. She smiled when she felt the vibrations the watch made when it struck the hour. At the time, young Helen did not know about Bell's devotion to teaching the deaf. All she knew was that he understood her signs, and she "loved him at once." His touch was tender and sympathetic. "I did not dream that that interview would be the door through which I should pass from darkness into light, from isolation to friendship, companionship, knowledge, love," she later wrote in *The Story of My Life*.[8]

Bell suggested that the Kellers write to Michael Anagnos, who had become the director of the Perkins School for the Blind, the position Dr. Howe had held before he died. At the institution, teachers were trained to educate the deaf and blind through Dr. Howe's methods. When Anagnos received the Kellers' letter, he reviewed the list of his recent graduates for a possible teacher for Helen. One name jumped immediately to mind. She had no experience as a teacher, either of the hearing and sighted, the blind, or the deaf and blind, but as a child, she had suffered from trachoma, an eye disease that had left her partially blind. Despite her visual impairment, she was his star graduate, well trained in Howe's methods. Brilliant, passionate, and persevering, 20-year-old Anne Sullivan seemed like the perfect match for the headstrong Helen.

Teacher

"The most important day I remember in all my life is the one on which my teacher, Anne Mansfield Sullivan, came to me," Helen Keller wrote in *The Story of My Life*.[1] On March 3, 1887, Helen, then nearly seven, stood on her front porch, waiting for something to happen but unsure of what it was. She could tell by the way her mother hurried around the house that someone important was coming. Outside, Helen tipped her face upward and let the warm beams of sunshine sprinkle on her cheeks.

Suddenly, she felt the vibration of approaching footsteps. Assuming it was her mother, Helen stretched out her hand. Someone else took it and pulled Helen into her arms. Knowing it was not her mother, Helen frantically struggled to free herself. The young woman trying to hold little Helen was Annie Sullivan, but Helen would come to know her as Teacher.

Sullivan was pleased when she saw that Helen was a healthy, sturdy girl. Because many blind children she had seen were physically frail, Sullivan had expected Helen to be a pale, delicate child. She studied Helen's face closely. "It is intelligent, but lacks mobility, or soul, or something," she wrote in her journal.[2] With Helen's chilly reaction to her hug, Sullivan decided that her first plan was to win the child's love.

Almost immediately, Sullivan realized that she had her work cut out for her. The next day, she witnessed one of Helen's wild tantrums firsthand. When Sullivan tried to calm her down, Helen kicked and flailed, knocking out one of Sullivan's front teeth. One morning at the breakfast table, Helen reached over to eat something off Sullivan's plate, as she did with other members of her family. Sullivan was appalled by Helen's rude table manners. When she refused to let Helen grab food from her plate, Helen flung herself onto the floor with screams, twists, and flops. Sullivan asked the Kellers to leave the room and locked the door behind them. Then she sat back down at the table and continued to eat her breakfast while Helen rolled around on the floor. At one point, Helen tried to jerk Sullivan's chair out from beneath her. Finally, Helen decided to get up and find out what Sullivan was doing. Sullivan let Helen feel that she was eating but would not let the child finger her food. Frustrated, Helen pinched Sullivan, who slapped the girl's hand each time she pinched. Curious as to why her mother let Sullivan slap her, Helen walked all around the table and found no one there. At last, she came back to her chair and began to eat her breakfast with her fingers. Sullivan gave her a spoon, which Helen threw on the floor. Determined to teach Helen good manners, Sullivan forced the little girl to pick it up. After a few minutes, Helen gave up fighting and finished her breakfast in peace. The ordeal was intensely emotional for Sullivan. After Helen finished eating, Sullivan let her go outside to play and went up to her room, where she threw herself on her bed. "I had a good cry and felt better," she wrote.[3]

Sullivan realized that, if she wanted to reach Helen, she would have to get the girl away from her family. For years, Captain Keller and Kate Keller had given Helen whatever she wanted. In order to teach Helen, Sullivan needed to discipline the unruly child. The Kellers agreed to let Sullivan use the small cottage next to the house, where the teacher and student would live. Sullivan had the furniture rearranged so the room would be unfamiliar to Helen. Then she took Helen for a carriage ride to make her believe they were going to a different place. Helen's family could visit them every day, but they were not allowed to let Helen know they were there.

The first day was a disaster. Helen kicked and screamed, refusing to let Sullivan touch her. That night, Sullivan had difficulty getting Helen to go to bed. Finally, after a two-hour struggle, Helen fell asleep. "I never saw such strength and endurance in a child," Sullivan wrote in a letter. "But fortunately for us both, I am a little stronger."[4]

Undaunted by Helen's tantrums, Sullivan persisted in teaching Helen to spell. Sullivan had begun this task as soon as she arrived at the Kellers' home. She placed a big rag doll on Helen's lap. Sullivan slowly spelled the word "d-o-l-l" in Helen's hand. At once, Helen became curious by this new finger play and tried to imitate it. When she finally succeeded in forming the letters correctly, she ran downstairs to her mother, held up her little hand, and made the letters for the word *doll*. At the time, Helen did not understand that she was spelling a word. She was simply making her fingers copy what Sullivan had done. In the

The water pump at Ivy Green that enabled Annie Sullivan to teach young Helen the word for water.

days that followed, Helen learned to spell many words, such as *pin*, *hat*, *cup*, *sit*, *stand*, and *walk*, but she still did not understand what they meant.

A SOUL SET FREE

On April 5, 1887, the cloud was lifted from Helen's mind, and a miracle occurred. While Helen was playing with a new doll, Sullivan also set the rag doll on Helen's lap and spelled *doll*. She tried to make Helen understand that the word *doll* applied to both objects. Earlier that morning,

Sullivan had tried to teach Helen the difference between the words *mug* and *water*. Sullivan showed Helen that a mug was something that held water, but Helen was confused. She thought both words meant the same thing. She did not know the word for drink, so whenever she spelled *mug* or *milk*, she made a pantomime of drinking something. That morning when Helen was having a bath, Sullivan tried to teach her the word water. She spelled "w-a-t-e-r" into Helen's hand. Later in the day, Helen and Sullivan stopped at the water pump between the house and the cottage. Sullivan made Helen hold a mug under the spout while she pumped. As the cold water poured over the top of the mug, Sullivan spelled "w-a-t-e-r" in Helen's free hand.

An expression of revelation lit Helen's face. She was coming to life—the mystery of language was revealed. This new understanding seemed to startle her, and she dropped the mug. At that moment Helen knew that "w-a-t-e-r" meant the cool liquid flowing over her hand. She later wrote, "That living word awakened my soul, gave it light, hope, joy, set it free!"[5] She spelled out *water* several times. Next, she pointed to the pump, urging Sullivan to tell her its name. Then, suddenly, she turned to Sullivan and asked for her name. Sullivan spelled "T-e-a-c-h-e-r." All the way back to the house, Helen learned the name of every object she touched. In just a few hours, she added 30 words to her vocabulary.

"It would have been difficult to find a happier child than I was as I lay in my crib at the close of that eventful day and lived over the joys it had brought me," Helen later wrote, "and for the first time longed for a new day to come."[6]

Helen remembered practically nothing about her life before Annie Sullivan arrived. "Before my teacher came to me, I did not know that I am. I was a phantom living in a no-world," she wrote about those earlier years of her life. "I had neither will nor intellect. I was carried along to objects and acts by a certain blind natural impetus. . . . My inner life, then, was a blank without past, present, or future, without hope or anticipation, without wonder or joy or faith."[7] For Helen, her life really began at age six, after she learned the meaning of words.

It took some time, but Helen slowly developed a more gentle personality. She began to understand that her actions affected the people around her. Several months after the incident at the water pump, Helen had another one of her tantrums. Sullivan was out of the room when it started. Viney, the child of one of the servants, noticed Helen filling up a glass with stones. Worried that the glass would break, she snatched it away. At once, Helen began to tear at Viney, scratching and biting her like a wild animal. Hearing the ruckus, Sullivan rushed in, grabbed Helen's hand, and asked her what had happened. Helen spelled "Viney—bad" and resumed her attack with slaps and kicks. Sullivan held both of Helen's arms tightly until she calmed down.

Later, Helen came into Sullivan's room looking sad. She wanted Sullivan to give her a kiss. Sullivan told her, "I cannot kiss naughty girl." Helen spelled back, "Helen is good, Viney is bad." Sullivan pointed out that Helen had struck and kicked Viney and hurt her. She explained that her behavior was naughty and refused to give Helen a kiss. Helen stood very still, her face flushed and troubled. It was obvious that there was a struggle going on in her mind. "Helen does not love teacher. Helen do love mother," she spelled. "Mother will whip Viney."[8] Sullivan told her that she should not talk about it anymore but think about it, and she left Helen to sit by herself.

At the dinner table, Helen became worried when Sullivan would not eat. Sullivan told Helen that her heart was sad and that she was not hungry. Helen began to sob and clung to Sullivan. Finally, she threw her arms around Sullivan's neck and said, "I will be good tomorrow. Helen will be good all days." Sullivan asked, "Will you tell Viney you are very sorry you scratched and kicked her?" Helen smiled, perhaps thinking she could get out of apologizing, and said, "Viney cannot spell words."[9] But Sullivan assured Helen that she would tell Viney for her. Helen agreed to say she was sorry and even let Viney kiss her.

That day, something in Helen seemed to change. She became unusually affectionate and sweet. Sullivan noticed what she called "a *soul-beauty* in her face,"[10] which she had not seen before. Month by month, the number of Helen's violent outbursts and physical assaults declined. She seemed to understand that people embraced her and her disability more openly when she was kind and cooperative. Years later, she explained how it felt to be blind and deaf in a world filled with people who could hear and see: "The experience of the deaf-blind person, in a world of seeing, hearing people, is like that of a sailor on an island where the inhabitants speak a language unknown to him, whose life is unlike that he has lived. He is one, they are many; there is no chance of compromise. He must learn to see with their eyes, to hear with their ears, to think their thoughts, to follow their ideals."[11] Helen keenly realized that it would make her life easier if she pleased those around her.

NO ORDINARY CHILD

Helen absorbed language and formed concepts of her surroundings with astounding speed. Her mind gobbled up knowledge like a ravenous lion. Within several months, she had learned hundreds of new words and began to read books written in Braille. (Braille is a system of writing and printing for blind or visually impaired people, in which varied arrangements of raised dots representing letters and numbers are identified by touch.) By the end of their first year together, Sullivan was spelling into Helen's hands stories from Homer's *The Iliad* and *The Odyssey*, as well as

William Shakespeare's plays and Bible stories. At eight years old, Helen was reading the works of great poets, such as Henry Wadsworth Longfellow, John Greenleaf Whittier, and Oliver Wendell Holmes.

Helen's ability to grasp complex ideas at such a young age was extraordinary. Sullivan, however, wanted to keep her pupil's genius-level intelligence somewhat of a secret. She worried that someone might try to exploit Helen if word about her accomplishments leaked out. In a report on Helen's progress to Michael Anagnos, director of the Perkins School for the Blind, she wrote, "Already people are taking a deep interest in Helen. No one can see her without being impressed. She is no ordinary child, and people's interest in her education will be no ordinary interest. . . . I shall write freely to you and tell you everything, on one condition: It is this: You must promise never to show my letters to any one. My beautiful Helen shall not be transformed into a prodigy if I can help it."[12]

Despite Sullivan's warnings, Helen's story was destined to reach the public. Anagnos decided to break his promise to Sullivan and introduce the world to this remarkable child. He titled the fifty-sixth annual report of the Perkins School "Helen Keller: A Second Laura Bridgman." In his report, he created a legend out of Helen by exaggerating her accomplishments.

Anagnos's report unleashed a storm of publicity, amazing readers across the country. Newspapers printed pictures of Helen reading Shakespeare or posed with her teacher, their faces so close together they almost melted into one. By age 10, Helen was world famous. People from all over Europe and the United States were enthralled with her progress. Queen Victoria of England was counted among her avid admirers.

While Helen's awakening was astounding, newspapers embellished her story, giving her almost supernatural

(continues on page 32)

LAURA BRIDGMAN

Born in 1829, Laura Bridgman was the most famous deaf-blind person of her time. Bridgman, like Helen Keller, was born with the ability to see and hear but lost them, along with her sense of taste and smell, after a bout of scarlet fever when she was just two years old.

It was Dr. Samuel Gridley Howe, the celebrated director of the Perkins School of the Blind in Boston, who changed Bridgman's life. Howe brought Bridgman to the school in 1837 and began to teach her English by using objects labeled with their names in raised letters. Bridgman soon realized the connection between the objects, letters, and communication and became the first deaf-blind person to learn language. Eager to learn, Bridgman continued to work with Howe and she eventually studied more complicated subjects, such as geometry, philosophy, and geography.

Howe wrote about Bridgman's remarkable intelligence and determination to learn in his annual report of the school. Word of his star pupil's accomplishments reached renowned writer Charles Dickens, who wrote about Bridgman in his book *American Notes*. It was Dickens's book that inspired the Kellers to contact Michael Anagnos, the new director of the Perkins School, for help and advice. Anagnos introduced the Kellers to Anne Sullivan, a recent graduate who was also a friend of Bridgman's. Sullivan taught Helen Keller how to communicate with the same methods Howe used while working with Bridgman.

Bridgman's education ended when she was 20 years old, and attempts to return her to the family farm in New Hampshire proved too difficult. She was welcomed back to Perkins and became a fearsome needlework instructor, intimidating many students throughout her years at the institute. She was almost 60 years old when she passed away. Her life clearly demonstrates how, despite seemingly insurmountable odds, disabilities can be overcome with determination and hard work.

A photo of Laura Bridgman, circa 1845. Helen Keller's mother was inspired to seek help for her own daughter after reading about how Bridgman was educated despite being unable to see or hear.

(continued from page 29)

abilities. Some articles claimed she could speak fluently, play the piano, and demonstrate geometry problems with her toy blocks. Others suggested that Helen and Sullivan could read each other's minds: After Helen fell asleep, Sullivan would mentally prepare the next day's lessons. When Helen awoke, she could supposedly recite the entire lesson from memory by spelling it out with her fingers.

Another person captivated by Helen's story was the man who set the Kellers on the path to the Perkins Institution— Alexander Graham Bell. He did not need Anagnos's report, though, to convince him that Helen was a special child. In November 1887, several months after the Kellers had visited him in Washington, D.C., he received a letter from Helen. It read:

> Dear Mr. Bell,
>
> I am glad to write you a letter. Father will send you a picture. I and Father and aunt did go to see you in Washington. I did play with your watch. I do love you. I saw doctor in Washington. He looked at my eyes. I can read stories in my book. . . .
>
> Good-by,
> Helen Keller[13]

Helen's letter was the first in what would become volumes of correspondence between the two of them. She wrote him frequently, often signing the letters, "Your loving little friend, Helen Keller."[14] Unlike other awestruck readers who devoured the sensational claims, Bell insisted that Helen was not a miracle, but rather, the result of brilliant instruction. He hoped her success would encourage other blind and deaf children to learn to read and write.

Apparently, Helen also thought she could use her fame to help other children. When she was 10 years old, a policeman shot her dog, Lioness. "I am sure they never could have done it if they had only known what a dear, good dog Lioness was," she said when she heard the news.[15] The heartbreaking story made its way into newspapers across the country and in Europe. Wanting to help, people began to offer her money for a new dog. Helen said that she did not want another dog but would accept the money on behalf of a poverty-stricken deaf, mute, and blind boy from Pennsylvania named Tommy Stringer. Helen had learned that Tommy wanted to go to Perkins to be educated, and she wanted to help. She wrote at least eight letters a day to people who were willing to give her money. She also wrote newspaper articles addressed to children.

Helen's generosity deeply moved the public. All over the world, people were convinced that Helen was no ordinary child. She had conquered what many believed to be impossible. Deprived of sight and sound, Helen had broken through her dark, silent barriers and learned to read, write, understand, and communicate with others. Helen, though, was about to take the miracle one step further. She wanted to learn how to speak with her voice.

The Wonder Girl

In March 1890, nine-year-old Helen Keller had never spoken a clear word in her life, except for the baby talk she babbled before her illness. She sat next to Mary Swift Lamson, Laura Bridgman's former teacher, who was spelling out some thrilling news into Helen's little hand. Lamson had just returned from a trip to Scandinavia. In Norway, she had met a deaf and blind girl who had been taught to speak with her lips. In *The Story of My Life*, Helen said that Lamson's words set her "on fire with eagerness."[1] Helen resolved that she, too, would learn how to speak and would not rest until Annie Sullivan found her a speech teacher.

Sullivan took Helen to see Sarah Fuller, the principal of the Horace Mann School for the Deaf in Boston,

Massachusetts. Fuller offered to teach Helen herself. She gently picked up Helen's hand and placed it lightly over her face, letting Helen feel the position of her tongue and lips when she made a sound. Eager to learn, Helen immediately imitated her motions. In just one hour, Helen had picked up six sounds of speech: M, P, A, S, T, and I. Although it took intense effort, Helen was thrilled when she uttered her first sentence: "It is too warm." No one other than Fuller or Sullivan, however, could understand a word of what she had said. Another teacher listening to the lesson described Helen's voice: "Her voice was to me the loneliest sound I have ever heard, like waves breaking on the coast of some lonely desert island."[2]

On the other hand, Helen was filled with delight. "No deaf child who has earnestly tried to speak the words which he has never heard—to come out of the prison of silence, where no tone of love, no song of bird, no strain of music ever pierces the stillness—can forget the thrill of surprise, the joy of discovery which came over him when he uttered his first word," she later explained.[3]

Later, Helen regretfully discovered that Fuller's method doomed her chances of ever speaking in a normal tone. Fuller and Sullivan had tried to build up Helen's speech before developing her vocal cords. Because Helen rarely spoke, her vocal cords were not trained for regular speech. Years later, Helen took three summers of speech lessons from Charles White, a distinguished teacher of singing at the Boston Conservatory of Music. With White's help, Helen improved the sound quality of her voice quite a bit.

Helen's popularity continued to grow. Newspapers hailed her as "the eighth wonder of the world." In Boston, she had been flooded with invitations to the homes of wealthy, influential citizens. While she was in town, Helen and Sullivan attended many of their parties. At age 10, Helen was a lovely young lady—five feet two, thin, and poised, with loose brown curls cascading over her shoulders. Her natural beauty and grace charmed everyone who met her. Her articulate intellect and stiff determination, however, impressed people the most. She would need that perseverance to carry her through her next obstacle.

After that first speech lesson in Boston, Sullivan continued to teach Helen back home in Tuscumbia, Alabama. Even after much work, Helen's voice was still incomprehensible to most people. Often, Helen had to put her sensitive fingers inside her teacher's mouth—sometimes so far down her throat that she gagged—in order to "feel" the vibrations of speech. "My work was practice, practice, practice," Helen later wrote. Even though she frequently felt discouraged, she stayed focused on her task. "My little sister will understand me now," she told herself and kept on trying. The thought of no longer being dumb—unable to speak—filled her with excitement. "I am not dumb now," she would say over and over again.[4]

During lessons, Helen learned a way to read other people's speech. By placing her middle finger on the nose, her forefinger on the lips, and her thumb on the throat of the person talking, she could feel the different vibrations that certain words made. In this way, she could "hear" what they said—just by paying attention to the vibrations. Helen's new technique allowed her to listen to almost anyone. She hoped that someday she could talk to people the way they talked to her.

Helen continued to work on her speech, which improved day by day. Although she was surrounded by dark silence, the love and kindness of what seemed like the entire world brought light into Helen's life. Her happiness, though, was about to be shattered by a birthday present that went horribly wrong.

"THE FROST KING" DISASTER

On November 4, 1891, Helen sent Michael Anagnos a story she had written, called "The Frost King," as a birthday present. "I little dreamed how cruelly I should pay for that birthday gift," she later wrote in her autobiography. When Helen wrote the story, the words and images came flowing to her fingertips. She composed sentence after sentence on her Braille slate. After she finished the story, she read it to Sullivan. At supper that evening, she read it to the entire family. Surprised she could write so well, one family member asked Helen if she had read the story in a book. The question threw Helen, because she did not remember ever reading anything like this story before. "Oh, no, it is my story," she said proudly.[5]

Helen carried her story to the post office. All the way, she was quite excited. Charmed by the whimsical tale, Anagnos published it in the Perkins School's alumni magazine. At the same time, "The Frost King" was printed in the *Goodson Gazette*, a weekly publication of the Virginia Institution for the Education of the Deaf and Dumb and Blind. The thought of being a published writer filled Helen with much pride.

Her moment of glory soon exploded into pieces, though. She learned that a story similar to "The Frost King," called "The Frost Fairies," by Margaret T. Canby, had already been published in a book. People began to accuse Helen of plagiarism—saying that she had copied the story and pretended she had written it. At that time, Helen eagerly absorbed everything she read without a thought of who had written it. She had a hard time separating her own ideas from the ideas she found in books. After she had been accused of plagarism, Helen read Canby's story and noticed the startling similarities in the plot and the language.

When Helen wrote "The Frost King," she believed it was an original story, the first of its kind. She was devastated

Helen Keller poses with Michael Anagnos, the director of the Perkins School for the Blind, circa 1890. When she sent him a story she had written, called "The Frost King," as a birthday present, she didn't realize that she had plagiarized much of it from a story by Margaret T. Canby.

to think she had been dishonest, even if it was by accident. "It made us feel so bad to think that people thought we had been untrue and wicked," she wrote despairingly in her diary. "My heart was full of tears, for I love the beautiful truth with my whole heart and mind."[6]

Helen felt that she had disgraced herself. Unable to figure out how this had happened, she racked her brain until she was exhausted, trying to recall if she had read the story before. Helen had written her story in the autumn, after taking a walk in the woods with her teacher. As they strolled through the trees, Sullivan described the leaves, twinkling like gems in colors of ruby, emerald, gold, and blaze orange. Helen thought the fairies must have painted them from jars of melted gemstones that King Frost kept in his castle. As it turned out, a worker at the Perkins School had read "The Frost Fairies" to Helen a long time ago. Although Helen honestly did not remember the story, the memory of the tale must have lingered in her mind and inspired her composition.

The incident deeply troubled and humiliated Anagnos. Several months after he printed the story, he had to run a retraction—a formal statement that takes back a previous statement—in the annual report to explain the mix-up. When he questioned Helen about the composition, she insisted that she had no idea such a story had been written before. At first, he believed her. Then one evening, a teacher from Perkins asked Helen a question about "The Frost King." Something in Helen's response made the teacher believe that Helen had known about Canby's story all along. She twisted Helen's words into a confession. When the teacher told Anagnos what Helen had said, he turned against Helen and Sullivan, accusing them of deliberately stealing the story.

Eleven-year-old Helen had to sit in front of a court of investigation, made up of teachers and officers of the Perkins School. The court asked Sullivan to leave the room so Helen could be questioned alone. Terrified, Helen tried to answer the questions carefully. Her heart thumped wildly in her chest until the very end of the examination. That night in bed, Helen cried herself to sleep. "I felt so cold," she recalled in her autobiography. "I imagined I should die before morning, and the thought comforted me."[7]

The members of the investigating committee split evenly; four believed she had not deliberately plagiarized the story, four did not. Anagnos broke the tie by siding with Helen. Throughout the following months, Helen received many messages of love and sympathy from both friends and strangers. Canby even wrote her a letter and told her, "Some day you will write a great story out of your own head, that will be a comfort and help many."[8] Eventually, most of the misery and bitterness of those days lifted off Helen's heart. Yet for a long time, when she wrote a letter—even to her mother—she was seized with a feeling of terror. She would spell a sentence over and over, just to make sure she had not read it in a book. At times, in the middle of writing a paragraph, Helen would say to herself, "Suppose it should be found that all this was written by some one long ago."[9] Sullivan helped restore Helen's confidence. "Had it not been for the persistent encouragement of Miss Sullivan," Helen later wrote, "I think I should have given up trying to write altogether."[10]

MOVING ON

"The Frost King" episode, although disturbing, taught Helen how to persevere through the trials of life. As the sting gradually disappeared, she emerged with a wider and truer knowledge of the world around her. With the help of a little traveling, she managed to move on with her education and rediscover happiness.

In March 1893, Helen and Sullivan traveled to Washington for the second inauguration of President Grover Cleveland. That same month, they visited Niagara Falls, on the border of New York and Canada. As Helen

Helen Keller and Annie Sullivan, around the time they began traveling together extensively. In 1893, they visited Washington, D.C., Niagara Falls, New York, and Chicago, Illinois.

stood on the landing over the falls, she felt the ground tremble beneath her. She was awed by the way the water rushed and plunged with wild fury at her feet. "It seemed as if it were some living thing rushing into some terrible fate," she later wrote. "One feels helpless and overwhelmed in the presence of such a vast force."[11]

During the summer of 1893, Helen and Sullivan visited the Chicago World's Fair (formally known as the World's

Columbian Exposition) with Alexander Graham Bell as their personal guide. At the exhibition, people flocked to see this famous deaf-blind girl who had made an astonishing breakthrough into the light of language and learning. To visitors, she was every bit as amazing as the invention of her companion. In the early 1890s, the telephone system was just being born. Only 200,000 to 300,000 people in the United States owned telephones, which Bell had invented in 1876. In March 1884, the first link in a national network, between New York and Boston, had been put into service. On October 18, 1892, Bell opened the first telephone line from New York to Chicago.

Unlike other visitors, Helen was allowed to touch all the exhibits. She took in all the grandness of the fair with her fingertips. During her tour, she got to touch a Viking ship, African diamonds, and French bronzes. At the Cape of Good Hope exhibit, she learned about the process of mining diamonds. Whenever she could touch the machinery in motion, she took advantage of it. By feeling the vibrations, she got a better sense of how the stones were weighed, cut,

IN HER OWN WORDS

In wandering around the Chicago World's Fair, Helen Keller had words of gratitude for Annie Sullivan. As related in *Helen's Eyes: A Photobiography of Annie Sullivan, Helen Keller's Teacher*, Keller said:

> My teacher described the beautiful scene to me so clearly and vividly that I do not think the picture which my imagination built could have been more vivid and real if I had seen it with my own eyes.

and polished. As she ran her hands over the French bronze statues, she was amazed that they felt so lifelike. "I thought they were angel visions which the artist had caught and bound in earthly forms," she commented.[12]

Bell went everywhere with Helen and Sullivan and described all the objects of greatest interest. At the electrical building, they examined telephones, phonographs, and other inventions. They also stopped at the anthropology exhibits. The relics of ancient Mexico captivated Helen. The crude stone tools that were the only record of that age fascinated her. "From these relics I learned more about the progress of man than I have heard or read since," she later wrote.[13]

Helen's experiences at the fair added many new words to her vocabulary. In the three weeks she spent there, she took a giant leap from a little girl's interest in fairy tales to the appreciation of the real living world. And yet, she wanted to know more.

Quest for College

By the time she turned 13, Helen Keller had already studied many subjects. She read the histories of Greece, Rome, and the United States. She owned a French grammar book in raised print and liked to compose sentences in her head using new words as she learned them, ignoring the rules as much as possible. She also took classes in arithmetic and Latin. At the same time, she kept working to improve her speech. She read aloud to Annie Sullivan and recited passages from her favorite poems, which she had put to memory. As Helen spoke, Sullivan corrected her pronunciation and helped her learn how to phrase and add voice inflection—an alteration of pitch or tone of the voice.

In the summer of 1894, Helen attended a meeting of the American Association to Promote the Teaching of

Speech to the Deaf, where she met two young men, John D. Wright and Dr. Thomas Humason, who were planning to open a school in New York City to teach oral language to the deaf. When they heard Helen speak, they felt certain that with new methods her voice might be trained to sound more natural. Perhaps, they thought, she could even be taught to sing. So in October, Helen and Sullivan traveled to New York City, where Helen enrolled in the Wright-Humason School for the Deaf.

After the first year, Helen's lip-reading and speech were still not what she had hoped. Her ambition was to speak like other people, but no matter how hard she worked, she could not quite reach her goal. At times, the disappointment caused Helen great distress. Still, she vigorously pursued her other studies. She used her time at the Wright-Humason School as a stepping-stone to her ultimate goal—college.

On August 19, 1896, while Helen and Sullivan were visiting friends in Massachusetts, Captain Arthur Keller suddenly died. When 16-year-old Helen heard the news, she was grief stricken and wanted to go immediately to Tuscumbia to be with her mother. Kate Keller, however, refused to let Helen attend the funeral, using the excuse that the intense heat and humidity of Alabama in the late summer would be too hard on Helen's health. More likely, Kate could not cope with her disabled daughter while dealing with her husband's death. Sullivan spelled Kate's decision into Helen's hand. At once, Helen burst into sobs. Her father was dead, and now her family was not letting her share their grief. Helen felt lonely and isolated. "He died last Saturday at my home in Tuscumbia, and I was not there," she wrote a friend. "My own loving father! Oh, dear friend, how shall I ever bear it?"[1]

In October, Helen entered the Cambridge School for Young Ladies in Massachusetts. Her classes there would prepare her for Radcliffe College, Harvard's college for women in Cambridge. When Helen was a little girl, she visited Wellesley College, a women's liberal arts college in Massachusetts. She surprised her friends by suddenly announcing, "Someday I shall go to college—but I shall go to Harvard!"[2] When her friends asked why she would not go to Wellesley, Helen told them that there were only girls there, not realizing that Harvard was then exclusively a men's college. From that day forward, the thought of going to college took root in her heart and grew into one of her most earnest desires. Moreover, she wanted to attain a degree side by side with seeing and hearing girls. Therefore, she chose to start at Cambridge—a school that would help her prepare for college-entrance exams—in hopes of one day fulfilling her childhood promise. It was her first step out into a world where she would be in direct competition with girls who could see and hear.

AT CAMBRIDGE

At 16, for the first time in her life, she got to spend time with girls her own age. "I joined them in many of their games," she wrote in *The Story of My Life*, "even blind man's bluff and frolics in the snow."[3] Helen took long walks with her new friends and got together with them to study and read. Some of the girls even learned how to speak to her so that Sullivan did not have to repeat their conversations. After Christmas, Helen's sister, Mildred, joined her as a student at the school. For the six months Mildred stayed at Cambridge, the sisters were hardly ever apart.

Sullivan was by Helen's side in every class, interpreting the teacher's lessons. At first, Sullivan thought that Helen would spend five years at Cambridge. However, she progressed so remarkably that, at the end of her first year, her course was shortened to three more years. Also, she was allowed to take part of her college-entrance examinations.

A photo of Helen *(left)* and her sister, Mildred, circa 1897. Mildred would follow Helen to the Cambridge School for Young Ladies in Massachusetts.

On June 29, 1897, she showed up for her first set of exams. In total, she had to pass a 16-course examination—12 exams of elementary courses and four exams in advanced courses. She had to pass five courses at a time in order for them to count. Helen tested in elementary and advanced German, French, Latin, and English, as well as Greek and Roman history. Sullivan was not allowed to be with Helen during the examinations, to make sure they did not try to cheat. Instead, the school's director, Arthur Gilman, agreed to take Sullivan's spot and learned the manual alphabet especially for the exams, so he could translate the questions for Helen. While the other students wrote their answers longhand, Helen was permitted to use a typewriter.

Much to Helen's delight, she passed every exam and received honors in German and English. "I think I may say that no candidate in Harvard or Radcliffe was graded higher than Helen in English," Gilman said. "No man or woman has ever in my experience got ready for these exams in so brief a time. How has it been accomplished? By a union of patience, determination, and affection, with the foundations of an uncommon brain."[4] Unfortunately, she did not repeat her spectacular scores the following year. She probably struggled through the exams because most of her courses were in math, not one of Helen's strong subjects. In addition, there was a delay in the printing of the Braille textbooks that would have helped her with her work.

Just before the books arrived, Gilman scolded Sullivan for pushing Helen too hard. Despite Helen's protests, he reduced her class load. He wanted Helen to stay at Cambridge three years longer. Wanting to enter college with the rest of her class, Helen felt discouraged and frustrated. In November, Helen spent three days in her room because she was not feeling well. Although she was not seriously ill, Gilman insisted that she was having a nervous breakdown from being overworked. Sullivan, knowing that Helen would quickly recover, argued with Gilman about Helen's condition. Because Gilman would not back down, Kate Keller withdrew Mildred and Helen Keller from the Cambridge School.

Helen continued her studies with a tutor, Merton S. Keith. From February to July 1898, Helen and Sullivan stayed with friends in Wrentham, a town located about 25 miles (40 kilometers) from Boston. Keith came out to Wrentham twice a week and taught Helen algebra, geometry, Greek, and Latin while Sullivan interpreted his lessons. In October, they returned to Boston, where Keith gave Helen lessons five days a week.

In this way, Helen could continue her preparation for Radcliffe without further interruption. She found it much easier to be taught alone rather than with the rest of the

DID YOU KNOW?

On the fiftieth anniversary of her graduation, Radcliffe College granted Helen Keller its Alumnae Achievement Award. Her alma mater also showed its pride in her by dedicating the Helen Keller Garden in her honor and by naming a fountain in the garden for Anne Sullivan Macy. Keller also received the Americas Award for Inter-American Unity, the Gold Medal Award from the National Institute of Social Sciences, the National Humanitarian Award from Variety Clubs International, and many other honors. She held honorary memberships in scientific societies and philanthropic organizations throughout the world.

Several countries recognized her work for the blind. Her worldwide accolades included the Order of the Southern Cross from Brazil, the Sacred Treasure from Japan, the Golden Heart from the Philippines, and the Gold Medal of Merit from Lebanon. In 1952, during the centennial commemoration marking the one-hundredth anniversary of the death of Louis Braille (the inventor of the Braille system), Keller was made a chevalier of the French Legion of Honor.

class. She could take her time, and the tutor could explain whatever Helen did not understand. Under Keith's tutelage, she absorbed the material much more quickly and did better work than she had ever done in school. She still struggled a little with mathematics, but Keith made studying algebra problems interesting.

In June 1899, Helen took her final examinations for Radcliffe College. The first day, she took tests in elementary Greek and advanced Latin. On the second day, she tested in geometry, algebra, and advanced Greek. Again, someone other than Sullivan read the exam papers to Helen. The geometry and algebra tests had been written in Braille for Helen, which caused some confusion. Helen was used to having the problems spelled into her hand and found the Braille hard to read. In addition, Keith had taught Helen to solve problems mentally, and for the tests, she had to show her work on examination papers. For this reason, her work was painfully slow, and she had to read the examples over and over again before she understood what she needed to do. Of course, Helen realized that the admissions board of Radcliffe did not understand how difficult it made the examinations for her to complete. "But if they unintentionally placed obstacles in my way, I have the consolation of knowing that I overcame them all," she later wrote.[5] She passed her exams, and her struggle for admission into Radcliffe had ended.

TELLING HER STORY

In the fall of 1900, Helen Keller entered Radcliffe College, becoming the first person with severe disabilities to enroll at an institution of higher learning. Keller began her studies with eagerness and excitement, but she soon learned that college was not the fairy tale she had imagined it would be. At Radcliffe, she was more deeply aware than ever of her blindness and deafness. Only one of her classmates knew finger language. In the lunchroom, Sullivan would spell the other girls' bright chatter into Keller's hand to help make her feel a part of the group. Still, Keller was painfully aware of the enormous gap between herself and her classmates, who were always kind to her. They even bought Keller a Boston terrier, which she named Phiz. Of all her professors, only one took the time to master manual finger language so he could communicate directly with Keller.

What seemed to bother Keller the most, though, was that she had less time for herself. Before, she always had time to think and reflect on the events of the day. In college, she was too busy to spend time in reflection. "One goes to college to learn, it seems, not to think," Keller later wrote in *The Story of My Life*.[6]

In the classroom, Keller felt so far away from the instructor it was as if he were speaking through a telephone. Sullivan would spell the lectures into Keller's hand as quickly as possible, leaving out unnecessary details or jokes to keep up the pace. She did not take notes during the lectures because her hands were busy listening. After class, she would jot down whatever she could remember. Keller later described how she felt during lectures: "The words rush through my hand like hounds in pursuit of a hare which they often miss."[7] Because no one like Keller had ever gone to college, few books for her courses were printed in Braille. Sullivan had to spell the text into Keller's hand.

Keller and Sullivan eventually developed a pattern, and schoolwork became less stressful. During Keller's second year at Radcliffe, her English composition teacher noticed her amazing literary talents. He encouraged her to write about the unique world in which she lived. The idea surprised Keller. She had always accepted other people's experiences as what it means to live. It never occurred to her that someone might find her own observations and experiences worthwhile. Since she arrived at Radcliffe, she had been desperately trying to be like everyone else and forget her limitations. Her English teacher's suggestion became a turning point. "Henceforth I am resolved to be myself, to live my own life, and write my own thoughts when I have any."[8]

Although writing was often difficult, Keller had a gift for words. At times, her English teacher thought she could write better than any student he had ever had in class. Before long, Keller's work came to the attention of the editors of the *Ladies' Home Journal*. They offered to pay her $3,000—a very impressive amount of money at the time—to write a five-part story of her life that they would publish in the magazine over five months. Sullivan encouraged Keller to sign the contract, but Keller soon found it was nearly impossible to keep up with her studies while writing her story. Adding to the pressure, the editors started to publish the articles before Keller had finished the complete manuscript.

Understanding Keller's distress, a friend came to her rescue and introduced her to John Albert Macy, an English instructor at Harvard and an editor of *Youth's Companion*. He agreed to learn the manual alphabet to help the 22-year-old Keller edit and complete her articles. While working with Keller, Macy realized that her articles could be expanded into a book. He shrewdly appointed himself her literary agent and made a deal with Doubleday. In March 1903, *The Story of My Life* was published—dedicated to Keller's good friend Alexander Graham Bell. In addition to being her autobiography, the book included selections from her journals and letters. She also described her education by including selected letters between Annie Sullivan and Sophia Hopkins, Sullivan's close friend from the Perkins School.

Although praised by critics, the book was not the best seller that Keller, Macy, and the editors at Doubleday had hoped it would be. In its first two years, it sold just 10,000 copies. Yet, in the years that followed, *The Story of My Life*

Helen Keller with Alexander Graham Bell, the inventor of the telephone, circa 1901. Keller honored the man who helped her and so many other deaf people by dedicating *The Story of My Life* to him in 1903.

became a classic that is still read by millions today. In fact, the New York Public Library named it one of the 100 most important books of the twentieth century in 1996.

On June 28, 1904, a day after her twenty-fourth birthday, Keller sat tall in her chair in the auditorium of Sanders Theater in Cambridge, Massachusetts. Shortly before the graduation ceremony, Keller gave a speech to the Radcliffe alumni: "College has breathed new life into my mind and given me new views of things, a perception of new truths and of new aspects of the old ones. I grow stronger in the conviction that there is nothing good or right which we cannot accomplish if we have the will to

WORKS BY HELEN KELLER

Although Helen Keller sometimes found writing difficult, she maintained a successful literary career that continued for more than a half century. The following is a list of Keller's books:

The Story of My Life, 1903

Optimism: An Essay, 1903

The World I Live In, 1908

The Song of the Stone Wall, 1910

Out of the Dark, 1913

My Religion, 1927

Midstream: My Later Life, 1929

Peace at Eventide, 1932

Helen Keller in Scotland, 1933

Helen Keller's Journal, 1938

Let Us Have Faith, 1941

Teacher: Anne Sullivan Macy, 1955

The Open Door, 1957

Helen Keller: Her Socialist Years, edited by Philip S. Foner, 1967

Pictured, Helen Keller in her graduation cap and gown. In June 1904, she graduated with honors from Radcliffe College, the first deaf and blind person ever to receive an undergraduate degree.

strive." In the same address, Keller spoke of her future with a sense of purpose: "The doors of the bright world are flung open before me and a light shines upon me, the light kindled by the thought that there is something for me to do beyond the threshold."[9]

Dressed in black robes, Keller and 95 classmates eagerly waited to receive their diplomas. When Keller's name was called, she gracefully walked up the steps of the stage, Sullivan's hand on her arm. A moment later, Keller's eager fingers gripped a paper that no other deaf-blind person had ever held up to that point—a bachelor's degree, and one with the honor of cum laude. (Cum laude is Latin for "with honors," as in, to graduate with honors or exceptional grades.) Seeing her student, Sullivan must have thought back to the first day she met Helen, then six, standing on her family's front porch, her face pale and blank, a prisoner of a dark and silent world. She had come so far since that day. She had blossomed into a beautiful young woman, filled with life, light, and happiness. In the yearbook, Keller's classmates recognized the weight of her achievement in verse:

> Beside her task our efforts pale,
> She never knew the word for fail;
> Beside her triumphs ours are naught,
> For hers were far more dearly bought.[10]

Curious Triangle

After graduation, Helen Keller and Annie Sullivan moved into their own house in Wrentham. "It's old-fashioned, roomy, and cheerful," Keller described. "I never had a room for all my books before."[1] That first summer, she loved to walk alone in the garden, which was overgrown with fruit trees, pines, and spruces. Her walks in solitude gave her a feeling of freedom. Usually she was unable to go out without a companion, but at home she could wander the garden whenever she chose, picking flowers and berries and sitting in the shade of the trees.

John Albert Macy visited Keller and Sullivan often. Ever since he had helped Keller publish *The Story of My Life*, he had acted as a sort of guardian for the women. Because of years of strenuous reading and studying for

Keller, Sullivan's already poor eyesight was deteriorating. The more time Macy spent with them, the more Sullivan became attracted to him. He was young, brilliant, and passionate. Although 11 years younger than Sullivan, he was captivated by her. They shared a superior intelligence that made them the perfect match.

As soon as Keller learned that her teacher was in love, she urged Sullivan to get married. Even though Macy had proposed, Sullivan was reluctant. She had devoted so much of her life to Keller, she felt as if she would be abandoning a dear friend. Keller was distraught over Sullivan's hesitation. "Oh, Teacher," she exclaimed, "if you love John, and let him go, I shall feel like a hideous accident."[2] Macy, however, had no intention of stealing Sullivan away from Keller. He loved them both and vowed never to separate them. Still, Sullivan refused to accept Macy's proposal unless he first received Keller's approval. "If you will ask Helen and if she is willing, I will think about it," Sullivan told him.[3]

So, one day, Macy went into Keller's study. Putting his hands on hers, he spelled out that he had proposed to Sullivan. Excited, Keller asked what her teacher had said. "She said—she spoke of you," Macy replied. Keller asked Macy if he loved Sullivan, to which he answered yes. "Does she love you?" Keller asked. Again, Macy answered yes. "Then, marry, of course," Keller said, "and I hope you will be very, very happy." Macy reassured Keller of her place in their lives. "We want you to be with us always," he told her. "You will be as dear and as necessary to Miss Sullivan as you have always been. We would not marry unless your life and hers were to go on just as before."[4] After he said these words, Keller smiled tenderly and thanked him. With Keller's consent, Sullivan said yes, and the couple announced their engagement on January 16, 1905.

On May 2, Macy and Sullivan were married at the Wrentham farmhouse. Although most brides wore beautiful, white, flowing gowns, Sullivan, being an older bride at 39, wore a conservative blue traveling dress with a white silk waist. That afternoon, the newlyweds left for New Orleans on their honeymoon. While they were away, Keller went back home to Tuscumbia to be with her mother. Being separated from Sullivan, even for a short time, was almost unbearable for Keller. After a few days, she began to feel lonely and isolated. As it turned out, Sullivan shared Keller's pain. After 18 years together, neither one of them knew how to live apart. The honeymooners dropped by Ivy Green for an unexpected visit. Keller was overjoyed at being reunited with her teacher: "It seemed like a dream, having them with me, reveling in the beauty of early summer in the Southland."[5]

The wedding must have caused Keller to think about love in her own life. Perhaps she even dreamed of getting married herself. She was resigned, however, to living a life without romance. Once, when she was in Washington visiting Alexander Graham Bell, the subject of marriage came up in their conversation. He asked Keller if she would consider finding someone to love. "No," she answered flatly, as if she had already accepted her fate. "I have fully made up my mind that a man and a woman must be equally equipped to weather successfully the vicissitudes of life. It would be a severe handicap to any man to saddle upon him the dead weight of my infirmities. I know I have nothing to give a man that would make up for such an unnatural burden."[6] Instead, she chose to experience marriage the same way she had experienced so many other things—through her beloved teacher.

The three of them lived together in a curious triangle of love and commitment. Keller now had a new companion who spelled into her hands with a fresh perspective and style. She could compare the stark differences in personality between Annie and John Macy just by the way they signed to her. She later wrote in her book *Midstream: My Later Life*, "And such a difference as there was in the way each talked! My teacher's

Here, Helen Keller *(left)* poses with Annie Sullivan and John Macy in Wrentham. After Sullivan married Macy, Keller lived with them and grew to love Macy dearly.

comments on scenes and news and people were like nuggets of gold, lavishly spilled into my hands, while her husband put his words together carefully, almost as if he were writing a novel." Keller and Macy became close friends. "Next to my teacher, he was the friend who discovered most ways to give me pleasure and gratify my intellectual curiosity."[7]

In time, Macy could lift Keller out of a depressed mood with a joke or a wisecrack, which he would communicate through their own special code. He stretched a wire and ropes almost a quarter of a mile along a field so that Keller could take a walk without hurting herself. She could just glide her fingers along the rope and take a quiet walk in complete freedom. With Macy's help, Keller wrote *The World I Live In*, which had first appeared as a series of essays in *Century* magazine under the title "Sense and Sensibility." Of all her books, *The World I Live In* was the most fascinating to the public. In it, she at last revealed the true nature of her inner world.

EDUCATION FOR ALL

Meanwhile, Keller had poured her energies into her own passion—a love for learning. While she was still at Rad-

IN HER OWN WORDS

The World I Live In provides a detailed account of Helen Keller's reality. In this passage from the book, she discussed being blind:

> To the blind child the dark is kindly. In it he finds nothing extraordinary or terrible. It is his familiar world; even the groping from place to place, the halting steps, the dependence upon others, do not seem strange to him. . . . Not until he weighs his life in the scale of others' experience does he realize what it is to live forever in the dark.

cliffe, one of her friends had convinced her that she was wasting time on books and study that would do nothing for others. She told Keller that she could accomplish more for humanity if she devoted her time to the education of children with afflictions like hers.

In October 1904, she and the Macys traveled to the St. Louis Exposition, celebrating the one-hundredth anniversary of the Louisiana Purchase. The exposition was originally scheduled to open in 1903, but it had taken longer than planned to organize. One of the events was an International Conference on the Deaf and Dumb. The conference featured a "Helen Keller Day," and those in charge invited Keller to speak. The president of the conference wanted her to talk about what was being done in the world to uplift people who struggle in unequal circumstances.

When the trio entered Congress Hall, it was packed to the doors. People stood on chairs, climbed onto the window ledges, and even stood on ladders outside to catch a glimpse of the famous "wonder girl." Dressed in a high-necked lace gown and a hat decorated with flowers, Keller delivered her speech with sufficient clarity and articulation. "Many have been invited here because of learning, skill, or achievement," she began. "I am here, not for what I have done, but what has been done for me—to raise me to the level of those that see and hear." She continued, "My evidence is of able men and women who have done what they could to unstop ears, open eyes, give speech to lips of the dumb and light to darkened minds."[8] Then Keller broadened her message by emphasizing the need to help the deaf, the blind, and the mute so they could enjoy the kind of life she had come to know. "This exposition symbolizes the will of the American people that there shall be an open way to education for all, no matter how humble their circumstances or how limited their capacity," she said.[9]

From that point forward, helping the blind became Keller's primary mission. She began what would become her lifelong work on their behalf. She served on the Massachusetts Commission for the Blind and wrote numerous articles on the prevention of blindness, the education of blind children, and the need for the state to provide training and jobs for the blind. In addition, she worked to raise public awareness on the plight of the adult blind—she believed their condition was almost hopeless because many had lost their vision when they were past the age of being educated and were unable to hold a job of any kind. She managed to persuade the editors of the *Kansas City Star* and the *Ladies' Home Journal* to publish her articles on a then-taboo subject—*ophthalmia neonatorum*, the major cause of blindness in newborns. Mothers suffering from venereal disease pass this preventable infection to their babies.

Keller believed that the devices used by the blind needed serious improvement. Not only were embossed (decorated with a raised design) books expensive, there was no unified system of embossed printing. As it was, various teachers of the blind supported their own theories as to which type was best, and the blind were not consulted. To read everything that had been printed for the blind, Keller had to master five different prints—New York Point, American Braille, European Braille, Moon type, and Boston Line Letter. She denounced the inconsistent materials. "A plague upon all these prints!" she once exclaimed.[10]

Regularly, Keller was asked to write articles, attend meetings, speak to legislatures, or visit schools. Alexander Graham Bell and others urged Keller to bring the problems of the deaf before the public as well. She refused, however, later explaining that "although I was as deeply interested in the cause of the deaf as I was in that of the blind . . . I found that it was not humanly possible to work for both the blind and the deaf at the same time."[11] Although at times it seemed like little was being done to help the deaf-blind of America, Keller continued to be optimistic.

BITTER SEPARATION

To Keller, her tinny, robotic voice was her ultimate nemesis. She felt that her lack of a strong, clear voice was her true handicap, even more than her blindness and deafness. She was always eager to try a new approach to fine-tune her voice. In 1910, Keller began to take voice lessons from Charles White, a singing teacher at the Boston Conservatory

A BOND WITH TWAIN

Throughout her lifetime, Helen Keller had the opportunity to meet many famous people. One of her most beloved friends was Samuel Langhorne Clemens (1835–1910), the author of *The Adventures of Huckleberry Finn* and *The Adventures of Tom Sawyer*, who was more commonly known by his pen name, Mark Twain. She first met Twain when she was 14 years old. The instant he clasped her hand, Helen could feel his genuine affection for her. Whenever she visited with Twain, he would tell her stories and make her laugh. He often led her through the house and yard, describing for her the scenery in the vivid language of a writer. "Try to picture, Helen, what we are seeing out these windows," he said during one winter visit. "We are high up on a snow-covered hill. Beyond, are dense spruce and firwoods, other snow-clad hills and stone walls intersecting the landscape everywhere, and over all, the white wizardry of winter. It is a delight, this wild, free, fir-scented place."*

Helen especially appreciated the way he never embarrassed her by saying how terrible it was not to see or how boring her of Music. White believed he could help Keller because he had created a special type of singing lesson for the deaf to increase the flexibility of their vocal cords. Because Keller wanted to give more lectures, she wanted to try to strengthen her voice.

At the same time, Keller and her teacher decided to fine-tune her appearance as well. For years, Keller had always been photographed in right profile to hide her left eye, which protruded and appeared obviously blind. If she were to go on a lecture tour, she would constantly be exposed to the merciless

life must be, always plagued by darkness. Once when they were together, another guest commented, "How dull it must be for her, every day the same and every night the same as day." Twain quickly jumped to correct him. "You're [darned] wrong there," he snapped. "Blindness is an exciting business, I tell you. If you don't believe it, get up some dark night on the wrong side of your bed when the house is on fire and try to find the door."** Instead of weighing Helen down with dreary sympathy, Twain liked to keep the mood light. One day, he offered to teach Helen how to play billiards. "Oh, Mr. Clemens, it takes sight to play billiards," she said. "Yes," Twain teased, "but not the variety of billiards that [some of my friends] play. The blind couldn't play worse."***

*Helen Keller, *Midstream: My Later Life*. Garden City, N.Y.: Doubleday, Doran & Company, 1929, p. 54.
**Ibid., p. 48.
***Ibid., p. 54.

A photo of Helen Keller with the author Samuel Clemens, better known as Mark Twain. Twain, who became her good friend, never pitied her for her condition.

gaze of the public. Therefore she had both eyes surgically removed and replaced with blue glass ones. The operation drastically improved her appearance, and she no longer had to be photographed from the right side. From then on, most photographs showed her looking straight ahead.

While the two women prepared for their tour, tensions at home had been building. Annie and John Macy had started to quarrel about her devotion to Keller. At first, Macy was understanding about the special relationship between this student and her teacher. After five years of living in this unusual situation, Macy became jealous of all the attention that his wife gave to Keller.

In January 1913, Keller appeared on a lecture tour for the first time. The first speech turned out to be a disaster. As soon as she began her speech, titled "The Heart and the Hand or the Right Use of Our Senses," she was seized by stage fright. Rattled, she forgot all of White's lessons and felt her voice run wild. Frantically, Keller tried to tone it down but ran off the stage in tears. Much to her surprise, the audience was sympathetic. Because of their enthusiastic response, she decided to line up more lectures for the spring.

That May, Macy sailed to Europe alone. He was gone for four-and-a-half months, hoping perhaps that the time away would ease some of the stress on his marriage. When he returned, though, nothing had changed. He and Annie continued to argue about her fixation on Keller at the expense of their relationship. He rented an apartment in Boston to put some distance between himself and the women. Although separated, the couple had not yet spoken of divorce, and sometimes the women joined Macy at the apartment. One night, after a particularly violent argument, Annie stormed out of the apartment, vowing never to return. Believing she had walked out on him forever, Macy consulted a lawyer and drew up papers charging Annie with the fault in declaring a divorce.

Even in the midst of marriage turmoil, the two women embarked on a Canadian lecture tour, taking along Kate Keller and leaving Macy alone at Wrentham. While they were away, the bickering between the Macys continued, through letters. When John accused Annie of never being a wife to him, Keller joined the bitter battle. She wrote several letters to Macy, defending Annie and pointing out how much they both loved him. Then, while the women were still on tour, Macy left a cigarette burning in the Boston apartment, which started a fire, ruining all of the belongings that Keller and Annie had kept there. Though the couple never officially divorced, the strange relationship triangle they maintained with Keller had come to an end. It seemed as though neither Keller nor Sullivan were destined for love. Keller could have never imagined she, too, would have her turn at love and heartbreak.

Little Island of Joy

During the autumn of 1913, Helen Keller, Annie Sullivan, and Kate Keller were constantly on the road. In January 1914, they started on their first coast-to-coast tour across the country. Social functions had always been trying for Keller. Even though she had been meeting and talking to strangers ever since she was eight, she never felt quite at ease in a crowd of people. The difficulty of meeting people through Sullivan's hand-spelling sometimes made Keller embarrassed and confused. Still, she knew that her lectures served an important purpose, so she tolerated shaking hands with hundreds of curious people whom she had never met and would probably never meet again.

Whenever it was possible, Keller visited a school for the blind or the deaf in the city where she was speaking.

Sometimes, though, her lecture schedule was so chaotic she could not. It deeply grieved Keller that she could not always make these visits, not only because it disappointed those who had invited her, but also because she was intensely interested in what was being done for the deaf and blind all over the country. Often she would receive letters from invalids who told her that they had read her books and wanted to see her, but they were unable to get to her lectures because of their physical limitations. Keller tried to find the time to visit these people.

The more people she encountered, the more ideas popped into her mind, changing her attitudes toward life. She had once believed that people were masters of their own fate and could mold their lives into any form they chose. She was convinced that, if a person wished strongly enough for anything, he or she could not fail to achieve it. Keller had overcome deafness and blindness enough to be happy in life, and she assumed that anyone who valiantly fought life's struggles could emerge victorious. Yet as she traveled around the country, she learned that life was more complicated than she had once thought. She had forgotten that she partly owed her success to the advantages of her family and the help of others. Suddenly she became aware that triumph was not within the reach of everyone and that opportunity often comes with education, family, and the influence of friends. Although at times things seemed hopeless, Keller held tightly to the belief that life could get better even in the face of defeat.

On their first tour, Keller, Sullivan, and Keller's mother journeyed throughout America, from coast to coast, and from Canada to the Gulf Coast, stopping in towns that dotted the muddy banks of the Mississippi along the way. On their next tour, in 1916, Sullivan's two new secretaries accompanied them, 29-year-old Peter Fagan and Polly Thomson, a slim and pretty young woman who had joined the household in 1914. As soon as they returned to

Wrentham in the fall, Sullivan developed a hacking cough and a sharp pain in her side. The doctors told Sullivan that she had tuberculosis—a deadly lung disease. In those days, doctors often advised patients with tuberculosis to spend time near areas of water. They believed that the humid air was good for the lungs. To help her recover from her illness, Sullivan's doctor suggested that she spend the winter months at Lake Placid in upstate New York. Since Sullivan was too sick to travel alone, Thomson would go with her. While Sullivan was away, Keller and her mother were to stay with her sister, Mildred, in Montgomery, Alabama.

As always, separation from Sullivan made Keller feel uneasy. "I saw more clearly than ever before how inseparably our lives were bound together," she wrote. "How lonely and bleak the world would be without her. Once more I was overwhelmed by a sense of my isolation."[1] On one of these lonely nights, before Keller and her mother had left for Alabama, Peter Fagan walked into the study, where Keller

DID YOU KNOW?

Helen Keller was an avid socialist. Socialism is an economic and political system that advocates the collective or government ownership and administration of the means of production and the distribution of goods. Communism is a form of socialism that abolishes private ownership entirely. Helen's 1913 book, *Out of the Dark*, tells the story of how she became a socialist—a political position that was neither popular in the United States at the time, nor in the years that followed. In fact, when Keller started to do work for the American Foundation for the Blind in 1923, some of the people at the foundation worried that her political views could hurt the foundation.

sat alone. Sitting down beside her, he lifted her hand in his own. He spoke in tender tones, trying to comfort her in the absence of her teacher. Then the conversation took a more serious turn, jolting Keller with words she had never heard before. "He was full of plans for my happiness," Keller wrote. "He said if I would marry him, he would always be near to help me in the difficulties of life."[2]

Keller was breathless. Never before had her heart been touched so deeply. "His love was a bright sun that shone upon my helplessness and isolation," she said. "The sweetness of being loved enchanted me, and I yielded to an imperious longing to be a part of a man's life."[3] She was so excited that she wanted to share her feelings with everyone she knew. Fagan, however, believed it was best to keep their love a secret, at least for the time being. Kate Keller did not like Fagan, perhaps because she suspected his affection for her daughter. The couple took long walks together in the woods, and Fagan often read softly to her. After a few weeks, they secretly went to the city registrar's office in Boston and applied for a marriage license.

Although Keller's heart longed to be with Fagan, she was troubled by his insistence on keeping their relationship a secret. Soon, though, the secret was discovered. One day, Helen's mother burst into her room. "What have you been doing with that creature?" Kate Keller asked about Fagan. "The papers are full of a dreadful story about you and him."[4] She was almost crazy with panic. She demanded that Helen tell her the truth. Feeling Kate's hostility toward her fiancé, Helen decided to protect him instead of confessing to their relationship. She pretended that she knew nothing. "Are you engaged to him?" Kate pressed. "Did you apply for a marriage license?"[5] Terrified of what her mother might say, Helen lied. She denied the whole affair.

Hoping to fool Kate, Helen reacted calmly to the news. She casually combed her hair, while Kate continued her tirade. Helen's cool behavior did not fool her mother, though. She already had proof. A servant had been spying on the couple and caught them kissing. Still, Helen insisted there was no truth in the newspaper articles.

Kate would take no chances. At once, she banished Fagan from the house. Helen was not even permitted to say good-bye to him. Before he left, however, he wrote her a quick note in Braille, telling her where he would be staying. Pressured by her mother, Helen publicly denied the engagement and even signed a written statement of denial through the family lawyer. Nevertheless, Helen and Fagan continued to find ways to see each other in private.

They realized that the only way they could be together was if they eloped. The couple came up with a dramatic plan. Helen and her mother were planning to go to Alabama on a boat that stopped at Savannah, Georgia. From Savannah, they were going to board a train for Montgomery. Fagan would kidnap her as she made her way from the boat to the train. The couple would make a run for Florida, where Fagan had a friend who was a minister. They could quickly get married before anyone had a chance to stop them. Unfortunately, the scheme was foiled when Kate discovered that Fagan had booked passage on the same boat. At the last minute, Kate changed their plans, returning the whole way to Montgomery by train. Fagan sailed alone.

Not easily deterred, Fagan showed up in Montgomery. One morning, Mildred spied Helen on the porch with a strange man. He was frantically spelling into Helen's hand. She immediately went to Kate and asked if this was Fagan, the man she had heard so much about. At once, Kate called to Mildred's husband, Warren, to get his gun. Still on the porch, Fagan stood up in front of the gun and professed his love for Helen, but Warren ran him off anyway. Helen's family thought that they had settled the matter once and for all, but they were wrong.

One night a while afterward, Mildred woke to a sound on the porch. She found Helen standing there, her bag packed, obviously waiting for her fiancé to whisk her away. Fagan never showed up, perhaps because he saw the commotion on the porch before he was able to snatch Helen. This incident marked the end of Helen's love affair.

Keller's hopes for love and marriage had been dashed. She had no choice but to return to her cloistered life. Rather than strike back in rage at her mother, Keller blamed herself for being foolish enough to fall in love. "I cannot account for my behavior," she later wrote. "As I look back and try to understand, I am completely bewildered. I seem to have acted exactly opposite to my nature."[6] Keller was likely talking about the way she had treated her family during her affair, when at one point she told them that she could not bear to live with them. Years later in *Midstream*, she wrote fondly of her memory. "The brief love will remain in my life, a little island of joy surrounded by dark waters," she confided. "I am glad that I have had the experience of being loved and desired. The fault was not in the loving, but in the circumstances."[7]

ON THE BIG SCREEN

In 1918, a popular historian named Francis Trevelyan Miller decided to write a movie based on Keller's life. Sullivan, Keller, and Miller wanted the film to be an accurate depiction of Keller's life, but the multimillionaire who put up the money pushed for a more commercial "thriller" approach. During the story conferences, tempers flared. Several times, Sullivan stormed out of the meetings in a rage. One female agent pointed out that Keller's life—though amazing and admirable—was not motion picture material. She had no lovers—none she would admit to at least—no exotic adventures, except those of her vivid imagination. In this agent's opinion, after Keller's emergence from silence and darkness, nothing dramatic happened to her.

The producers struggled to figure out how to portray her almost singular life on film. They decided to focus on Keller's imagination, on her ability to separate her consciousness from space and time and somehow transport herself to other places, both in the present and in the past. Still, they had to give her a boyfriend—even if he was not real. As a young girl, she had once gone to a library with Sullivan and read a Braille book about ancient Greece. She told Sullivan how, while she was reading, she had suddenly been taken far away to Athens. Miller decided that Keller's lover should be the mythical Greek hero Ulysses, also known as Odysseus.

Scenes were filmed about their romance, which took place in Keller's mind. In the movie, after Keller graduated from Radcliffe College, a new shot reveals her dressed in a seductive gown, seated outside a Greek temple. During the scene, she is wooed by the bare-chested Ulysses, the survivor of a shipwreck on the island of Aeaea, home of the enchantress Circe. Their love leads to a lusty kiss. In the filming of the scene, Keller is played by a stunt actress.

The movie business seemed like a crazy world to Keller. She laughed every time Sullivan described the Ulysses scene to her. Another scene Keller found comical was a sequence in which "Knowledge" (played by a stunt-woman) and "Ignorance" (played by a male giant) had a fistfight for her mind as an infant at the entrance of the "Cave of Father Time." There was also a bedroom scene, in which Keller revealed to the public that she could do her own hair. In the final scene, which Keller also found ridiculous, she had to ride on a white horse and blow a trumpet, representing a sort of Joan of Arc leading the people of the world to freedom. Filming the scene turned out to be a frightening experience when Keller's horse suddenly reared. If it had not been for a brave cameraman who quickly jumped to her rescue, she might have been bucked off and seriously injured.

Perhaps the most disturbing scene for Keller to film was one in which she appeared at a formal banquet. All of her friends, both living and dead, were seated with her around the table. "I felt as if I had died without knowing it, and passed on to the other world, and here were my friends who had gone before coming to greet me," Keller later described. "But when I grasped their hands, they seemed more substantial than I had imagined spirit hands would be. Moreover, they did not resemble the hands of the friends they were impersonating."[8] Keller felt a little shocked every time one of them spoke to her. When the actor playing Mark Twain made a witty remark, she did not know whether to laugh or to cry. At the end of the scene, Keller said, "Eighty thousand blind people are unhappy and unhelped, and in the present state of society it is impossible to give them the opportunities they should have. . . . Millions of human beings live and die without knowing the joy of living. . . . Let us resolve now and here to build a saner, kindlier world for everybody."[9]

The movie, *Deliverance*, was an early docudrama (a filmed dramatization of events that are based on fact), but was in essence a hodgepodge of scenes that combined actual footage of Keller, symbolism, and a whimsical plotline. It was heralded as a real melodrama of Keller's life, but included none of her real-life struggles—her thwarted love affair, her complex relationship with her teacher, the way the people in her life fought to control her. Still, it was an important historical piece, capturing Keller as a beautiful, shining young woman—dancing, reading Braille, writing letters, and strolling in the garden with her mother. Despite

A movie poster for *Deliverance*, the fanciful silent film account of Keller's life, in which she starred.

her limitations, Keller came across as fearless. In one scene, a pilot offers her a ride in his two-seater plane, and without hesitation, Keller agrees. "Was I afraid?" she later wrote. "How could fear hold back my spirit, long accustomed to soar? . . . Up, up, up I climbed the aerial mountains until I felt rain-clouds spilling their pearls upon me." The pilot took her through a series of dips. "I felt in them, as it were, organ music and the sweep of the ocean," she described. "I had never had such a satisfying sense of physical liberty."[10]

Unsurprisingly, Keller did not fit into the racy Hollywood scene. She quickly discovered that filmmaking was far from the glamorous life she had envisioned. She stood on the movie set, almost unrecognizable in a blond wig and white makeup. A dresser adjusted the collar of her pale pink dress, as Polly Thomson spelled the director's instructions into the palm of her hand. After Thomson finished and stepped away, Keller waited for the "tap, tap, tap" vibrations, signaling to her that the film was rolling. The only real pleasure she found in Hollywood was horseback riding with Thomson every morning. "Some of the happiest hours of my life were spent on the trails of Beverly Hills," she wrote.[11]

In December, after the film was finished, Keller, Sullivan, and Thomson returned to Forest Hills, New York. They had bought a small, odd-looking house with a dozen peaks and angles. They jokingly called it "Castle on the Marsh." In August 1919, they were set to attend the opening of *Deliverance* but discovered that an actors' strike had closed most of the theaters on Broadway. Keller's picture was still scheduled to open, but it was being used as a strike-breaker—a way to pressure actors into going back to work. Furious and refusing to be used for someone else's agenda, Keller did not attend her own opening. Instead, she joined a protest march with the striking actors and actresses.

In truth, Keller did not really want to attend the movie anyway. When Sullivan spelled a description of the final version of the film into Keller's hand, Keller realized that it was far from the noble message she had envisioned. The public must have agreed. Despite a few glowing reviews, *Deliverance* was a box-office failure. Now without money, Keller had no choice but to accept another kind of stage offer.

In February 1920, Keller and Sullivan opened a vaudeville show to a full house in Mount Vernon, New York. Vaudeville shows featured dancers, comedians, singers, acrobats, and performing animals, as well as what were known in the business as "freak and odd acts." A freak act featured someone who had been on the front page of the newspapers for some crazy, tabloid-like incident. For example, one such act was "The Human Tank," a man who swallowed live frogs and threw them up alive. (Eventually his act was banned for its cruelty to the frogs.) Freak acts surged for only a short time. As soon as the novelty wore off, the audience was no longer interested, and the acts were replaced with something new. In contrast, an odd act was booked for many seasons. Odd acts ranged from opera singers to poets. Keller's story was considered an odd act, and performing it onstage would earn Keller and Sullivan some much-needed money.

In vaudeville, they could perform in one place for an entire week, instead of traveling from town to town as they did on the lecture tours. Their presentation was a great deal shorter as well. Each afternoon and evening, they appeared onstage for a brief 20-minute act. Keller loved the theater, with its rush, glare, and noise. She could dress up in a sequined evening gown with a chiffon train and wear theatrical makeup, which she learned to put on herself after a few lessons. Most importantly, vaudeville paid much better than writing or lecturing, and it turned out to be the answer to their chronic financial woes. In fact, Keller and Sullivan were among the highest-paid

(continues on page 84)

EXCERPT FROM HELEN KELLER'S VAUDEVILLE ACT

Vaudeville acts often used quick-witted humor to entertain audiences. In Keller's act, the audience would ask her questions, and she would respond with answers that reflected her beliefs and opinions. Her quick responses were not as spontaneous as one might think. Typically, Sullivan and Keller wrote a list of the questions that were most often asked and rehearsed answers. The questions mirrored the issues of the day: Prohibition (the national ban on the sale and manufacture of alcohol that lasted from 1920 to 1933), government topics, war, and the Ku Klux Klan. Here are some excerpts from Keller's vaudeville show:

Question: "Which is the greatest affliction—deafness, dumbness, or blindness?"

Keller: "None."

Question: "What then is the greatest human affliction?"

Keller: "Boneheadedness."

Question: "Do you think any government wants peace?"

Keller: "The policy of governments is to seek peace and pursue war."

Question: "Can you feel moonshine (homemade alcohol)?"

Keller: "No, but I can smell it."

Question: "What do you think is the most important question before the country today?"

Keller: "How to get a drink."

Question: "What do you think of Soviet Russia?"

Keller: "Soviet Russia is the first organized attempt of the workers to establish an order of society in which human life and happiness shall be the first importance, and not the conservation of property for a privileged class."

Question: "Who are the most unhappy people?"

Keller: "People who have nothing to do."

Question: "What have you enjoyed most in life?"

Keller: "Overcoming difficulties."

Question: "What do you think of [President] Harding?"

Keller: "I have a fellow-feeling for him; he seems to be as blind as I am."

Question: "Do you think America has been true to her ideals?"

Keller: "I'm afraid to answer that; the Ku Klux Klan might give me a ducking."

Question: "What is your idea of happiness?"

Keller: "Helpfulness."

Question: Who is your favorite heroine in real life?"

Keller: "Kate O'Hare, because she was willing to go to jail for her ideal of world peace and brotherhood."

Question: "Do you think the voice of the people is heard at the polls?"

Keller: "No, I think money talks so loud that the voice of the people is drowned."

Question: "What is the greatest obstacle to universal peace?"

Keller: "The human race."

Question: "What is the slowest thing in the world?"

Keller: "Congress."

Question: "Do you desire your sight more than anything else in the world?"

Keller: "No! No! I would rather walk with a friend in the dark than walk alone in the light."*

---

*Joseph P. Lash, *Helen and Teacher: The Story of Helen Keller and Anne Sullivan Macy*, New York: Delecorte Press, 1980, pp. 496–497.

Helen Keller and Annie Sullivan in 1920, during the period in which they were performing their vaudeville act.

IN HER OWN WORDS

Because Helen Keller could not see or hear, her other senses were especially sensitive, and she used them to "see" the world around her. In *Midstream: My Later Life*, she described how fine-tuned her sense of smell had become:

> I usually know what part of the city I am in by the odors. There are as many smells as there are philosophies. I have never had the time to gather and classify my olfactory impressions of different cities, but it would be an interesting subject. I find it quite natural to think of places by their characteristic smells.
>
> Fifth Avenue, for example has a different odor from any other part of New York or elsewhere. . . . It may sound like a joke to say that it has an aristocratic smell; but, it has, nevertheless. As I walk along its even pavements, I recognize expensive perfumes, powders, creams, choice flowers, and pleasant exhalations from the houses. In the residential section I smell delicate food, silken draperies, and rich tapestries. Sometimes, when a door opens as I pass, I know what kind of cosmetics the occupants of the house use. I know if there is an open fire, if they burn wood or soft coal, if they roast their coffee, if they use candles, if the house has been shut up for a long time, if it has been painted or newly decorated, and if the cleaners are at work in it. I suggest that if the police really wish to know where stills and "speakeasies" are located, they take me with them. . . .
>
> I know when I pass a church and whether it is Protestant or Catholic. I know when I am in the Italian quarter of a city by the smells of salami, garlic, and spaghetti. I know when

(continues)

(continued)

we are near oil wells. I used to be able to smell Duluth and St. Louis miles off by their breweries, and the fumes of the whiskey stills of Peoria, Illinois, used to wake me up at night if we passed within smelling distance of it.

In small country towns, I smell grocery stores, rancid butter, potatoes, and onions. The houses often have a musty, damp aura. I can easily distinguish Southern towns by the odors of fried chicken, grits, yams, and cornbread, while in Northern towns the predominating odors are of doughnuts, corned beef hash, fishballs, and baked beans.

(continued from page 79)

performers on the vaudeville stage, headlining for $2,000 a week at the Palace and other theaters.

Keller adored the stage so much that little could keep her away. Even when her mother died suddenly in 1921, she decided the show must go on. She got the news only two hours before the performance. "Every fiber of my being cried out at the thought of facing the audience," Keller recalled, "but it had to be done."[12] With her mother gone, Keller only had Sullivan. Then, later in the year, while performing in Toronto, Canada, Sullivan collapsed with a severe case of the flu. Thomson, Sullivan's assistant, took her place onstage. Although Sullivan recovered for a time, by the following year, severe bronchitis prevented her from appearing with Keller. She could barely speak above a whisper. From that point on, Thomson began to take over more of Keller's care. Sullivan was slowly fading from Keller's life.

Bringing Light to the World

Annie Sullivan was going blind. When she was five years old, she had suffered a violent case of trachoma. A series of operations had restored her sight, but throughout her life, she suffered from attacks that gradually ate away her vision. In 1929, Sullivan's right eye, which had developed a cataract, became so painful that it had to be removed. Then a cataract affected her left eye as well, drastically dimming her vision. By 1934, her sight had almost completely failed. Now, Polly Thomson was caring for both Helen Keller and Sullivan.

All of a sudden, the roles had been reversed. Sullivan was the pupil, and Keller the teacher—trying to ease Sullivan's fear of blindness. It was difficult for Sullivan to accept blindness, having been able to see almost her entire life. Keller never remembered seeing, and she understood the difference. "All my life I have lived in a dark and silent world. I seldom think of my limitations, and they never make me sad, but to see the light failing in another's eye is terrible, especially when one is unable to do anything about the tragedy," Keller wrote.[1]

Keller tried to teach Sullivan to read Braille. Sullivan found it difficult, however, because the system had changed since she first taught it to Keller. "Helen is and always has been thoroughly well behaved in her blindness as well as her deafness, but I am making a futile fight of it, like a bucking bronco," Sullivan confessed.[2]

While Sullivan was struggling with her failing sight, Keller was finding new ways to fulfill her life. In 1923, she took a position as the national and international counselor for the American Foundation for the Blind. While performing in vaudeville, Keller and Sullivan were offered jobs as fundraisers. Now they began to speak at occasional meetings. The foundation needed someone like Keller to get the public's support. She symbolized the very essence of their cause—that the blind needed opportunity, not charity. Given that opportunity, people with disabilities can triumph over anything. As expected, people flocked to the meetings. At first, the gatherings were held at the homes of wealthy socialites, but the meetings soon required more space. Keller and Sullivan began to speak in churches and lecture halls. By the spring of 1924, Keller had given up her vaudeville act and devoted her time to the foundation.

In 1927, Keller took a leave from lecturing to write *Midstream: My Later Life*, an autobiography of her later life. She had been postponing the book, because it took a lot of slow, deliberate work to write in Braille. In *Midstream*, Keller faced the reality that someday her teacher would no longer be with her. She confessed, "I peer with a heavy heart into the years to come. Hope's face is veiled, troubling fears awake and bruise me as they wing through the dark. I lift a tremulous prayer to God, for I should be blind and deaf in very truth if she were gone away."[3]

The writing of *Midstream* put a tremendous strain on Keller. She rewrote the book at least four times—composing and revising in Braille. After she was finished, Keller announced, "I just want to say this: There will be no more books. I put the best years of my childhood and youth into *The Story of My Life*. I have put the best years of my womanhood into *Midstream*."[4] Years later, however, Keller would write several more books and numerous magazine articles.

From 1932 to 1936, Keller and Thomson spent much time traveling abroad with a sickly Sullivan, who was confined to her bed almost all the time. On the morning of October 20, 1936, Keller sat at her teacher's bedside, gently holding her hand. At 7:30 A.M., the woman who had devoted almost her entire life to Keller passed away. She was 70. Toward the end of her life, Sullivan remarked, "I have been compelled to

IN HER OWN WORDS

Because of her inability to communicate well in her early years, Helen Keller probably had a greater appreciation for words than most people. She once said, as cited in *Helen's Eyes: A Photobiography of Annie Sullivan, Helen Keller's Teacher*:

> What a marvelous thing is language! How seldom we give it thought! Yet it is one of the most amazing facts in life. By means of the spoken or written word, thought leaps over the barrier that separates mind from mind.

pour myself into the spirit of another and to find satisfaction in the music of an instrument not my own and to contribute to the mastery of that instrument by another." Sullivan gave most of her life to her beloved student, but she never regretted it. "We do not, I think, choose our destiny," she said. "It chooses us."[5]

In 1931, *Good Housekeeping* had chosen Keller as one of the 12 greatest living American women. The magazine admitted that perhaps Keller and Sullivan should have been named together as one entry. If it had not been for Sullivan, Keller would probably have still been living in a dark and meaningless world. Still, to the very end, Sullivan insisted that Keller took her opportunity and gained an independent personality. A short time before Sullivan died, a friend tried to pay her a compliment by saying, "Helen would be nothing without you." Sullivan did not see it that way. "Then, my life has been wasted," she replied.[6]

On November 3, Keller traveled to Washington, D.C., where Sullivan's ashes were placed in the vault in the Chapel of St. Joseph of Arimathea at the National Cathedral. At the time of Sullivan's death, the bishop sent word to Keller that the cathedral would grant Sullivan the right to be interred at the cathedral. He let her know that she would also be offered the honor. Annie Sullivan was the first woman to be given this honor for her achievements as one of the great teachers of all time.

Now 56, Keller would have to live without Sullivan, but her disability still prevented her from living alone. With Sullivan gone, she relied on Polly Thomson and other people for her needs. After 22 years as Sullivan's assistant, Thomson quickly stepped up as Sullivan's replacement in Keller's life.

AROUND THE WORLD

Keller continued to gain public support for her cause. By 1937, 30 states had established commissions for the

A photo of Polly Thomson and Helen Keller in 1950. After Annie Sullivan's death in 1936, Thomson became Keller's chief companion.

blind. She had also raised international awareness and had begun ambassadorial tours on behalf of the blind in other countries. Sometimes the U.S. government funded these trips. Other times, these tours were sponsored by foreign governments.

One such trip occurred in the spring of 1937, when Keller and Thomson sailed for Japan, at the request of the Japanese government, to raise money for the blind and the deaf. This trip was the first of Keller's three tours in Japan, and over her time there, she developed a close relationship with the Japanese people. Before Sullivan died, Keller had learned that, of the 100,000 deaf people and 160,000 blind people in Japan, only 4,000 of them were being educated. One of Sullivan's dying requests was that Keller do her best to help them.

Before she left, Keller received a letter from President Franklin Delano Roosevelt, wishing her the best on her tour. "I feel confident that your presence will prove a lasting inspiration to those Japanese laboring under physical handicap," Roosevelt wrote.[7] Keller wrote back to thank Roosevelt for his kind words. She had long been a supporter of Roosevelt, who was an advocate for the disabled. Roosevelt's concern for the handicapped grew out of his own experience. In August 1921, at age 39, Roosevelt was stricken with polio, a disease that left him paralyzed from the waist down. Through intense physical therapy, he gradually recovered, but he was still left permanently disabled, able to walk only short distances with canes, leg braces, and support from his sons. It is no surprise, therefore, that Roosevelt came to empathize with people who were dealt a difficult hand in life. Roosevelt once said, "Anything Helen is for, I am for."[8] In 1935, Keller used her influence with Roosevelt to plead for government support for the Talking Book program, which would help educate blind people. Because of Keller's endorsement, Roosevelt offered his support for the project.

In Japan, Keller delivered 97 lectures in 39 cities. She raised 35 million yen for the blind and deaf and successfully encouraged the Japanese people to abandon their old myths and superstitions about the blind. She persuaded the people to start a nationwide movement to help the disabled in their country. The Japanese had never seen anyone like Helen Keller. While she was there, they treated her like royalty.

In 1939, Keller and Thomson moved into a home near Westport, Connecticut. Here she rarely needed to be guided around. As she had done for many years, she could

THE DEAF-BLIND TODAY

Today few deaf-blind people suffer from Helen Keller's lifelong condition. That is, few people are completely deaf and blind from an early age. Treatments for life-threatening childhood illnesses, such as meningitis and scarlet fever, have decreased the chances of permanent damage. Therefore the simultaneous onset of blindness and deafness seldom occurs.

The education of deaf-blind people has changed since the days of Keller and Annie Sullivan. In the early 1930s, Dr. Gabriel Farrell, the director of the Perkins School for the Blind, changed the policy of a deaf-blind student being assigned his or her own private teacher. If Keller were to be taught today, she would be instructed by several teachers. However, Sullivan's innovative teaching methods of talking into Keller's hand and instructing her in natural environments are still considered the best ways to teach a deaf-blind person.

Despite Keller's dream of a better future for the disabled, the blind are still struggling to achieve equality and find employment. Of the 9.7 million people who are blind or visually impaired in the United States, only 26 percent of them, age 21 to 64, hold jobs.

take a bath alone, pick out her clothes, dress herself, and fix her hair. Keller spent much of her day alone, meditating, working in her book-lined study, or strolling along a walk that had been built for her. In the summer, she tended her flower beds every morning and picked blueberries, able to tell by touch when they were ripe.

Keller continued to help other handicapped people throughout the world. During World War II, she became a symbol of hope to thousands of blinded, deaf, and disabled soldiers. In 1943, she visited 70 army and navy hospitals throughout the country. At first, many of the veterans thought she was like other celebrities who had been sent to visit them—just there to cheer them up and shower them with false hope. Yet, as they listened to her words through Thomson, they quickly realized that this woman was encouraging them to deal realistically with their limitations. She explained that although they would never enjoy their old freedom, they could still find satisfaction through friends, family, books, and accomplishments.

For Keller, her hospital tour in 1943 was "the crowning experience of my life. A drop of sweetness stole into my grief over the paralyzed as they tried to put their wasted arms around me, not always successfully, but their wish was a benediction I shall treasure forever."[9] During one visit, a soldier even offered her one of his eyes if it would make her see.

After the war, she promoted services for soldiers who had been blinded in the fighting. And she continued to be a crusader for the deaf and blind all over the world—taking nine global tours from 1946 to 1957, visiting 34 countries in all. These tours were sponsored by the American Foundation for the Overseas Blind, a sister organization of the American Foundation for the Blind. Many of her visits resulted in schools being started for the blind and deaf.

During her first tour, in 1946, a fire destroyed her home in Connecticut. The news deeply affected Thomson, but Keller was less troubled by it. A new home was rebuilt on the site.

By the 1950s, many people in the world considered Keller the greatest living American woman, a symbol of human perseverance and courage. In 1954, her birthplace, Ivy Green, in Tuscumbia, Alabama, was placed on the National Register of Historic Places. *The Unconquered*, a biography film of her life, was released that same year. Some years later, the documentary was renamed *Helen Keller in Her Story*. Another production of her life called *The Miracle Worker* was performed both onstage and onscreen.

ALONE

By 1954, Thomson's health had deteriorated. She was plagued with chronic rages followed by depression. She had a tumor removed from her brain, but it did not change her mood swings. On the morning of September 26, 1957, Keller and Thomson were upstairs in Keller's study, practicing speeches for several events. Around 11 o'clock, Thomson suggested that they go downstairs for an early

IN HER OWN WORDS

Everyone could stand to heed Helen Keller's counsel. She once said, as cited in *Helen Keller: A Life*:

Life is a daring adventure or nothing.

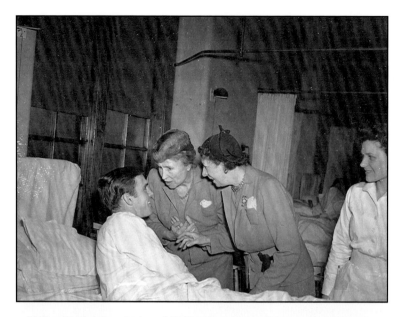

Helen Keller *(center)* and Polly Thomson visit the bedside of a young wounded soldier. During her hospital tour in World War II, one wounded soldier offered her one of his eyes, if it would allow her to see.

lunch so they could spend the afternoon rehearsing the speeches. They started downstairs, and when they reached the kitchen door, Thomson suddenly halted and shouted, "John!" Then she started trembling and had difficulty breathing. After a few minutes, Thomson acted as if she were fine. She went over to the stove and started to turn the burners on and off, repeating, "Put it on the stove." Keller asked her, "What am I to put on the stove, Polly?"[10] Thomson would not answer her.

Thomson continued to act confused and disoriented. Keller did not know what to do. If she left Thomson's side, she might not be able to find her again. Suddenly Thomson fell to the floor. Keller could feel Thomson's pulse throbbing wildly. She instantly knew her companion had suffered a stroke. Keller crouched next to Thomson on the floor and waited for someone—anyone—to arrive. After two-and-a-half hours, the postman finally came to the door. At last, Thomson could get to the hospital.

Although Thomson recovered from her first stroke, she continued to suffer from repeat attacks. On March 21, 1960, Thomson died at the age of 76. She had helped take care of Keller for 46 years. At 80 years old, Keller was alone. Yet it was a sort of freedom she had never experienced. For the first time in her life, she was surrounded by ordinary people who demanded nothing of her. After Keller's death, Winifred Corbally, a devoted nurse and companion, took care of Keller until her last days.

In the later years of her life, Keller did little work for the American Foundation for the Blind and spent more time with her relatives in Montgomery. In October 1961, Keller suffered a slight stroke. Other minor strokes followed. For the next seven years, Keller, who also had diabetes, was confined to a wheelchair and her bed. Despite her condition, she continued to be recognized for her work. In 1964, President Lyndon B. Johnson awarded her the Presidential Medal of Freedom, the nation's highest civilian award. A year later, she was elected to the Women's Hall of Fame at the New York World's Fair. Then, in May 1968, Keller suffered a heart attack. On Saturday, June 1, Helen Keller died at Arcan Ridge, her home in Westport, Connecticut, at the age of 87.

Following Keller's cremation, a funeral service was held in Washington, D.C., at the National Cathedral. In addition to many well-known Americans, the public memorial was attended by many deaf and blind people. Later, in a private ceremony at the Chapel of St. Joseph of Arimathea, the urn holding Keller's ashes was deposited next to those of Annie Sullivan and Polly Thomson.

All of her life, Helen Keller envisioned a better world, where social fairness prevailed. It was a dream not only for the disabled, but for all. "The only lightless dark is the night of ignorance and insensibility," she wrote. "We differ, blind and seeing, one from another, not in our senses, but in the use we make of them, in the imagination and courage with which we seek wisdom beyond the senses."[11]

CHRONOLOGY

1880   Helen Keller is born on June 27 in Tuscumbia, Alabama, to Kate and Arthur H. Keller.

1882   Helen becomes seriously ill, most likely with scarlet fever, leaving her deaf and blind.

1887   Annie Sullivan arrives on March 3 in Tuscumbia to be Helen's teacher.

1891   Helen sends a story she wrote, called "The Frost King," to Michael Anagnos, director of the Perkins Institution for the Blind, as a birthday present; after Anagnos publishes the story, Helen is accused of plagiarism.

1894   Helen and Sullivan attend the Wright-Humason School for the Deaf in New York City.

1896   Captain Keller dies; Helen enrolls in the Cambridge School for Young Ladies in Massachusetts.

1900   Helen enters Radcliffe College.

1902–1903   Helen writes and publishes her autobiography *The Story of My Life*.

1904   Keller and Sullivan purchase a farm and seven acres in Wrentham, Massachusetts; Keller graduates from Radcliffe.

1905   Sullivan marries John Albert Macy.

1906   Keller is appointed to the Massachusetts Commission for the Blind.

1908   *The World I Live In* is published.

1914	Polly Thomson is hired as Sullivan's assistant.
1916	Keller and Peter Fagan secretly apply for a marriage license; the relationship is thwarted before they can marry.
1919	Keller stars in *Deliverance*, a film based on her life.
1920	Keller and Sullivan start a vaudeville act.
1921	Kate Keller dies.
1923	Keller begins to speak for the American Foundation for the Blind.
1929	Keller publishes *Midstream: My Later Life*.
1936	Annie Sullivan dies on October 20.
1937	Keller visits Japan to raise money for the Japanese blind and deaf.
1943	Keller tours military hospitals.
1946–1957	Keller undertakes nine global tours during these years, giving lectures on behalf of the disabled.
1960	Polly Thomson dies on March 21.
1961	Keller suffers her first stroke and retires from public life.
1968	Keller dies on June 1 in her Connecticut home at the age of 87.

NOTES

CHAPTER 1: TRIUMPH OVER SILENCE

1. Helen Keller, *Midstream: My Later Life*. Garden City, N.Y.: Doubleday, Doran & Company, 1929, p. 90.
2. Helen Keller, *The Story of My Life*. New York: Signet, 2002, p. 46.
3. Royal National Institute of Blind People, "The Life of Helen Keller." http://www.rnib.org.uk/xpedio/groups/public/documents/publicwebsite/public_keller.hcsp#P127_16427.

CHAPTER 2: FROM LIGHT INTO DARKNESS

1. Keller, *The Story of My Life*, p. 5.
2. Ibid., p. 6.
3. Dorothy Herrmann, *Helen Keller: A Life*, New York: Alfred A. Knopf, 1998, p. 11.
4. Keller, *The Story of My Life*, p. 8.
5. Ibid., p. 13.
6. Ibid., p. 13.
7. Herrmann, *Helen Keller: A Life*, p. 24.
8. Keller, *The Story of My Life*, p. 15.

CHAPTER 3: TEACHER

1. Ibid., p. 16.
2. Herrmann, *Helen Keller: A Life*, p. 42.
3. Ibid., p. 43.
4. Ibid., p. 43.
5. Keller, *The Story of My Life*, p. 18.
6. Ibid., p. 18.
7. Herrmann, *Helen Keller: A Life*, p. 46.
8. Ibid., p. 47.
9. Ibid., p. 49.
10. Ibid., p. 49.
11. Ibid., p. 49.

12. Joseph P. Lash, *Helen and Teacher: The Story of Helen Keller and Anne Sullivan Macy*. New York: Delacorte Press, 1980, pp. 61–62.
13. Herrmann, *Helen Keller: A Life*, p. 66.
14. Ibid., p. 66.
15. Ibid., p. 66.

CHAPTER 4: THE WONDER GIRL

1. Keller, *The Story of My Life*, p. 44.
2. Herrmann, *Helen Keller: A Life*, p. 77.
3. Keller, *The Story of My Life*, p. 45.
4. Ibid., p. 46.
5. Ibid., p. 48.
6. Herrmann, *Helen Keller: A Life*, p. 80.
7. Keller, *The Story of My Life*, p. 50.
8. Ibid., p. 51.
9. Ibid., p. 55.
10. Ibid., p. 51.
11. Herrmann, *Helen Keller: A Life*, p. 90.
12. Keller, *The Story of My Life*, p. 57.
13. Ibid., p. 58.

CHAPTER 5: QUEST FOR COLLEGE

1. Herrmann, *Helen Keller: A Life*, p. 110.
2. Keller, *The Story of My Life*, p. 63.
3. Ibid., p. 66.
4. Herrmann, *Helen Keller: A Life*, p. 116.
5. Keller, *The Story of My Life*, p. 72.
6. Ibid., p. 73.
7. Ibid., p. 74.
8. Herrmann, *Helen Keller: A Life*, p. 131.
9. Lash, *Helen and Teacher*, p. 315.
10. Ibid., p. 314.

CHAPTER 6: CURIOUS TRIANGLE

1. Ibid., p. 319.
2. Ibid., p. 323.
3. Ibid., p. 325.
4. Ibid., p 325.
5. Herrmann, *Helen Keller: A Life*, p. 146.
6. Ibid., pp. 146–147.
7. Ibid., p. 152.
8. Lash, *Helen and Teacher*, p. 322.
9. Ibid., p. 322
10. Herrmann, *Helen Keller: A Life*, p. 177.
11. Ibid., pp. 177–178.

CHAPTER 7: LITTLE ISLAND OF JOY

1. Herrmann, *Helen Keller: A Life*, p. 196.
2. Ibid., p. 196.
3. Ibid., p. 196.
4. Ibid., p. 196.
5. Ibid., p. 196.
6. Ibid., p. 198.
7. Keller, *Midstream: My Later Life*, p. 182.
8. Ibid., p. 215.
9. Ibid., pp. 215–216.
10. Ibid., p. 217.
11. Ibid., p. 218.
12. Ibid., p. 228.

CHAPTER 8: BRINGING LIGHT TO THE WORLD

1. Herrmann, *Helen Keller: A Life*, p. 232.
2. Ibid., p. 232.
3. Keller, *Midstream: My Later Life*, pp. 343–344.
4. Herrmann, *Helen Keller: A Life*, p. 241.

5. Marfé Ferguson Delano, *Helen's Eyes: A Photobiography of Annie Sullivan, Helen Keller's Teacher*. Washington, D.C.: National Geographic, 2008, p. 60.

6. Herrmann, *Helen Keller: A Life*, p. 257.

7. Ibid., p. 271.

8. Ibid., p. 272.

9. Ibid., p. 289.

10. Ibid., p. 314.

11. Ibid., p. 345.

BIBLIOGRAPHY

Ferguson Delano, Marfé. *Helen's Eyes: A Photobiography of Annie Sullivan, Helen Keller's Teacher*. Washington, D.C.: National Geographic, 2008.

Herrmann, Dorothy. *Helen Keller: A Life*. New York: Alfred A. Knopf, 1998.

Keller, Helen. *Helen Keller's Journal*. Bath, England: Cedric Chivers, 1973.

———. *Midstream: My Later Life*. Garden City, N.Y.: Doubleday, Doran & Company, 1929.

———. *My Religion*. New York: Pyramid Books, 1974.

———. *Teacher: Anne Sullivan Macy*. Garden City, N.Y.: Doubleday & Company, 1956.

———. *The Open Door*. Garden City, N.Y.: Doubleday & Company, 1957.

———. *The Story of My Life*. New York: Signet, 2002.

———. *The World I Live In*. New York: The Century Company, 1908.

Lash, Joseph P. *Helen and Teacher: The Story of Helen Keller and Anne Sullivan Macy*. New York: Delacorte Press, 1980.

FURTHER RESOURCES

BOOKS

Garrett, Leslie. *Helen Keller: A Photographic Story of a Life*. New York: DK Publishing, 2004.

Gibson, William. *The Miracle Worker*. New York: Alfred A. Knopf, 1957.

Sullivan, George. *Helen Keller: Her Life in Pictures*. New York: Scholastic, 2007.

———. *In Their Own Words: Helen Keller*. New York: Scholastic, 2001.

WEB SITES

American Foundation for the Blind
http://www.afb.org

Helen Keller International
http://www.hki.org

Helen Keller Services for the Blind
http://www.helenkeller.org

Ivy Green: The Birthplace of Helen Keller
http://www.helenkellerbirthplace.org

PICTURE CREDITS

INDEX

ABOUT THE AUTHOR

RACHEL A. KOESTLER-GRACK has worked as an editor and writer of nonfiction books since 1999. Throughout her career, she has worked extensively with historical topics, ranging from the Middle Ages to the American Colonial era to the civil rights movement. In addition, she has written numerous biographies on a variety of historical and contemporary figures. Rachel lives with her husband and daughter in the German community of New Ulm, Minnesota.